1 0 S T E P S T O

Successful
Strategic Planning

Susan Barksdale and **Teri Lund**

ASTD
PRESS

Alexandria, Virginia

ASTD Press is an internationally renowned source of insightful and practical information on workplace learning and performance topics, including training basics, evaluation and return-on-investment (ROI), instructional systems development (ISD), e-learning, leadership, and career development.

Ordering information: Books published by ASTD Press can be purchased by visiting ASTD's website at store.astd.org or by calling 800.628.2783 or 703.683.8100.

Library of Congress Control Number: 2006932460

ISBN-10: 1-56286-457-2
ISBN-13: 978-1-56286-457-6

ASTD Press Editorial Staff
Director: Cat Russo
Manager, Acquisitions & Author Relations: Mark Morrow
Editorial Manager: Jacqueline Edlund-Braun
Editorial Assistant: Kelly Norris
Copyeditor: Christine Cotting
Indexer: April Davis
Proofreader: Kris Patenaude
Interior Design and Production: UpperCase Publication Services, Ltd.
Cover Design: David Cooper

United Graphics LLC, Mattoon, IL, www.unitedgraphicsinc.com

CONTENTS

Let's face it, most people spend their days in chaotic, fast-paced, time- and resource-strained organizations. Finding time for just one more project, assignment, or even learning opportunity—no matter how career enhancing or useful—is difficult to imagine. The *10 Steps* series is designed for today's busy professional who needs advice and guidance on a wide array of topics ranging from project management to people management, from business planning strategy to decision making and time management, from return on investment to conducting organizational surveys and questionnaires. Each book in this new ASTD series promises to take its readers on a journey to basic understanding, with practical application the ultimate destination. This is truly a just-tell-me-what-to-do-now series. You will find action-driven language teamed with examples, worksheets, case studies, and tools to help you quickly implement the right steps and chart a path to your own success. The *10 Steps* series will appeal to a broad business audience from middle managers to upper-level management. Workplace learning and human resource professionals along with other professionals seeking to improve their value proposition in their organizations will find these books a great resource.

P R E F A C E

Most successful organizations practice strategic planning. These organizations benefit not only from having a plan, but also from the planning process itself. The plan is the road map to success, and the planning process unites organizational leadership and enhances the communicating of critical company information. Today's volatile marketplace demands that employees, work groups, and organizations have a clear understanding of their roles, the products and services they offer, and the processes they use to navigate the continually changing waters they sail. A strategic plan that is directly related to group and individual planning provides an opportunity to create an outcome-based organization culture.

In the face of rapid change, organizations have realized they cannot compete on a global basis without a strategic plan that encourages innovation and creates knowledge internally and that builds customer loyalty to their products and services. A strategic plan provides the path an organization will take in the future (whether it will stay on course or follow a different direction than in the past); the predictions of how the marketplace, customer base, and product line will change or react to the future; and the calculated risk that the organization will need to bear to move in that direction. During strategic planning, organizations set their priorities for the next two to five years and identify how major resources will be allocated. If done correctly, the strategic plan should be a document that motivates employees to achieve the plan's stated goals and tactics. When realignment or redirection takes place, it is the strategic plan that explains the change in direction and refocuses the organization's efforts by redefining the organizational goals and major tactics.

But how do you develop a successful plan? The *10 Steps to Successful Strategic Planning* is process driven and comprises the following 10 steps:
1. laying the foundation for the plan
2. scanning the business environment

3. collecting relevant data
4. analyzing collected data
5. stating mission, vision, and values
6. prioritizing needs and identifying risks
7. designing and validating tactics
8. prioritizing tactics and resources
9. documenting and communicating the plan
10. maintaining the plan.

Strategic planning provides a plethora of opportunities for an organization, such as facilitating discussion and analysis of past performance using a methodical approach, providing a method to prioritize performance needs and organization goals, supplying information that will assist in prioritizing resources, and enabling the organization to be proactive rather than reactive and therefore more in control. Developing a plan will enable your organization to

◆ ensure the products and services delivered to its customer base are consistent and of high quality

◆ appraise past performance and identify successes and areas for future improvement

◆ create a consistent, sharp marketing message that promotes realistic expectations about the organization

◆ promote better use of resources (people, things, time, and finances)

◆ manage customer expectations

◆ limit resource investment in activities that do not provide results

◆ encourage individuals to be more proactive and resourceful in problem solving through understanding how the strategy affects their responsibilities and accountabilities

◆ resolve internal performance problems by clarifying expectations and standardizing performance

◆ strengthen its culture by motivating employees to embrace professional ethics and practices.

The uses of a strategic plan vary as much as one organization varies from another. Organizations use strategic plans to direct business planning, to allocate funding during budgeting, to communicate with employees, to form the basis for new-employee orientation materials, and to aid individual performance planning, among many other uses. Because a strategic plan is the foundation for the organization's future it should be used for organizational performance planning and evaluation, goal setting and assessment, communication, and financial planning.

10 Steps to Successful Strategic Planning is part of the 10-Step Series and was written to provide you with a proven process and tool set to create a strategic plan. We hope that the tools contained in this book will guide you each step of the way in building a successful strategy. As you implement the strategic plan, you and your organization will continue to benefit from your strategic thinking.

Susan Barksdale and Teri Lund
November 2006

INTRODUCTION

Mistakes are costly—so costly they can force out of business an organization once seen as an industry leader and powerhouse. Strategic plans help alleviate mistakes because they support a company's ability to

- ◆ apply resources where they are needed and "ignore" practices that don't need to be changed
- ◆ prioritize needs and tactics in a way that provides more benefit for the cost
- ◆ evaluate *realistically* if a tactic can be achieved within the timeframe identified and with the resources that were to be allocated
- ◆ examine internal and external forces and business drivers that will affect the organization's customers, products, and, ultimately, its business practices
- ◆ link the identified goals with the tactics it will take to achieve those goals.

This book, *10 Steps to Successful Strategic Planning,* provides a framework to use in developing a strategic plan quickly and efficiently. This book outlines a practical process and offers methods and tools that you can use to develop a strategic plan in a short timeframe. Case examples in every chapter illustrate each step in the process and show how other companies have approached the process. The case studies feature organizations of various sizes and styles—perhaps one just like yours.

Use whichever parts of this book you need. For example, if you are in the midst of creating a strategic plan, you can focus on articulating the mission, vision, and values of the strategic plan, identified in Step 5. Or if you have already collected the data and must analyze them quickly and meaningfully, you can use the methods and tools outlined in Step 4: Analyzing the Collected Data.

This book, *10 Steps to Successful Strategic Planning*, brings you the proven and current techniques for strategic planning; it makes specific methods, case examples, checklists, worksheets, and other tools available for immediate use in your organization. Most important, it helps you develop a plan that provides direction and guidelines quickly. This workbook will show you how to

- ◆ create a strategic plan to guide the initiatives and tactics in your organization that will meet organizational goals and objectives
- ◆ enhance others' involvement in the planning effort
- ◆ formulate a practical process for developing a strategic plan for organizations and individual departments or units
- ◆ use methods, tools, and outlines for developing a strategic plan
- ◆ create a culture that encourages employees to become strategic business partners
- ◆ integrate trends and new tactics into your strategic planning process.

Target Audiences

Organization leaders and others who are responsible for initiating and leading the development of a strategic plan, whether for the whole organization or a department or unit, will find this book most valuable.

If your job involves strategic planning, and you are interested in quickly providing direction to your team, aligning your services and products with your organization's business, and being able to market what you offer to management, employees, your customers, and your business partners, then *10 Steps to Successful Strategic Planning* is for you. Whether your organization is one of the *Fortune* 100, a not-for-profit, or a small startup, the tools and worksheets provided here will decrease the time and effort needed to develop a strategic plan.

Structure of the Workbook

This workbook will help you get the strategic planning process done quickly and successfully. Each section describes one of the 10 specific steps for creating a performance-driven strategy. Here is an overview of the 10 steps as presented in the workbook:

- **Step 1: Laying the Foundation** addresses why strategic planning is important, and includes tools to define the scope of the plan; identify outcomes, goals, and objectives; and determine a plan development timeline. Identifying key participants, mapping sponsorship, gaining commitment, and initiating the marketing for the plan are also addressed in this step.
- **Step 2: Scanning the Business Environment** kicks off the strategic plan development. Included are tools for scanning the business environment and questions to use in gathering necessary information. This step also covers a process for identifying current and future business drivers.
- **Step 3: Collecting Relevant Data** explains why it's crucial that you gather germane data before you develop a functional strategy. Tools and tables that provide types of data, data sources, and uses for the data collected are supplied in this step, as is a process for planning your data gathering and for using preexisting information sources. Finally, there are tools to help you determine the validity and reliability of the collected data.
- **Step 4: Analyzing the Collected Data** addresses how to examine the data collected for the strategic plan and fo-

cuses on coding and sorting data and completing calculations. Tools and worksheets help you assemble and review the data and determine if the key findings are valid.

◆ **Step 5: Stating Mission, Vision, and Values** emphasizes the importance of defining mission, vision, and values statements as part of your strategic planning. We've included guidelines for creating your statements and for setting organization objectives.

◆ **Step 6: Prioritizing Needs and Identifying Risks** explains how to establish criteria for ranking business needs and identify risks so you can define the tactics you'll pursue. Included in this step are tools to help rank-order alternatives and to manage risks, and there is a decision matrix that will make it easier to choose the tactics for your plan.

◆ **Step 7: Designing and Validating Tactics** shows you how to evaluate your possible tactics to ensure their compatibility with the mission and company objectives you've established. The tools and worksheets in this step help you identify desirable business outcomes and measures to ensure success. You'll discover a process to align your chosen tactics with your plan's original scope and objectives. How to create a tactical plan and assign executive accountability also are addressed.

◆ **Step 8: Prioritizing Tactics and Resources** provides tools to help you define the resources your tactics demand and determine when those resources will be needed to deliver your tactics.

◆ **Step 9: Documenting and Communicating the Plan** offers a plan outline along with tips for documenting the plan. You'll also find helpful our six-step process for creating and initiating a communication strategem.

◆ **Step 10: Maintaining the Plan** discusses the importance of keeping the plan current and defines the maintenance steps and actions that accompany those steps. In this step we also give you a process for forecasting the timeline and the personnel you will need to maintain your plan.

Laying the Foundation

OVERVIEW

Defining the scope

Identifying outcomes, goals, and objectives

Setting the timeframe

Choosing key players

Mapping advocacy

What is the future of the organization? What practices and procedures will be necessary for operating in the future? What issues face the organization? How does the organization communicate its vision, mission, strategic goals, and tactics to its employees, partners, customers, and stakeholders? How and when are important decisions made? Whether an organization is large or small, for profit or not-for-profit, volunteer-based, academic, or governmental, a strategic plan should answer these questions.

A strategic plan is central to a company's ability to make critical business decisions and is the springboard for operational planning. It serves as a communication vehicle for the company's mission, vision, values, and long-term objectives; and it inspires and excites employees, customers, partners, shareholders, and others about the organization as it operates today and where it is headed in the future. A strategic plan directs and predicts how the customer base and product line will react or change in the future, and it identifies risks the organization will have to bear if it's to move in the desired direction.

During the strategic planning process, organizations usually set priorities for the next two to five years and identify how major resources will be allocated. If done correctly, a strategic plan will motivate employees to achieve the company's goals. When organizational realignment or redirection takes place, a strategic plan explains the change in direction and refocuses the organization's efforts by redefining organizational goals and tactics.

An organization's business plan takes the initiatives and tactics borne of the strategic plan and drills down to operational details to identify how the company's goals and objectives will be met. The strategic plan drives the business plan, and the business plan in turn dictates the management functions of the organization—how marketing, finance, human resources, and other areas will achieve the outcomes identified in the strategic plan. In other words, the business plan translates the strategic plan into action.

POINTER

A strategic plan is central to a company's ability to make critical business decisions and is the springboard for operational planning.

The first step in *10 Steps to Successful Strategic Planning* is to lay the foundation for developing a strategic plan. In this step you'll find the information, tools, and worksheets to help you initiate the planning process. These are the topics we'll cover:

- ◆ defining the plan's scope
- ◆ identifying plan outcomes, goals, and objectives
- ◆ determining the timeframe for developing the plan
- ◆ identifying key participants in developing the plan
- ◆ mapping advocacy for the plan
- ◆ gaining commitment for developing the plan
- ◆ initiating the marketing of the plan.

Let's consider three case examples to show how the first step in strategic planning operates in a range of organizations.

Case Examples: Laying a Foundation

Our examples show how a technology company, a not-for-profit organization, and a human resource (HR) department used the first step in the 10-step process to initiate their strategic planning efforts.

Kicking Off the Process at an Established Tech Firm

New Technology is a *Fortune* 500 company that supplies technology through a network of franchises and resellers who serve end users. The firm has a strategic plan that is a little more than two years old, but senior management believes that changes in technology and the marketplace demand a new strategy, and employee satisfaction surveys have indicated a need for strategic reevaluation. Earlier employee surveys and a review of the marketplace have shown that employee service levels are declining with employee satisfaction, and customer satisfaction is suffering as a result. The organization is quickly losing market share to its competitors. Is employee dissatisfaction the only reason? A reformulated strategic plan has to address these issues and identify what is needed to revitalize the organization.

By following the activities suggested in Step 1, New Tech is able to identify these three desired outcomes for the strategic plan:

1. Determine what the company needs to do to become technically competitive.
2. Determine if employee dissatisfaction is the only factor in the decrease in customer satisfaction, or if there are other contributing factors.
3. Strengthen its understanding of what the competition is doing to increase its customer and employee satisfaction.

Setting the Stage for Successful Planning

Art on the River is a grassroots event-based effort to raise money for programs to benefit children in the local area. In the past, no thought was given to the future of Art on the River, but this year a charitable foundation has offered to match the funds raised through the organization's event. Realizing that this takes the event to a new level, a member of the steering committee has suggested creating a strategic plan that looks at how funds were allocated this year and how they should be allocated in the future. Once the members of the steering committee grasped the benefits of strategic planning, they understood that their event needed a well-defined scope to assist in raising and allocating funds.

By defining their intended outcomes, goals, and objectives early on, they were able to excite several foundations into contributing to Art on the River and working as business partners in establishing its final strategic plan.

Starting to Plan at the Department Level

ThoughtWare manufactures components that support e-technology. Its HR department provides training to the end-use customer who buys ThoughtWare's products. The company has gone through a major reorganization as part of its new strategic plan and has dramatically changed the product line it offers its customers. As a result, the HR group is uncertain who its customer is and how it can best support the business in the current environment. After an initial two-hour strategy-planning meeting, HR planning leaders have identified a set of questions to put before ThoughtWare's executives. The answers to these questions will help gain advocacy for HR's department-level strategic plan and will provide additional information that the planning team can use to successfully create its strategic goals.

Defining the Scope

The first action in strategic planning is *defining the scope of the plan*. Questions such as, What outcomes are desired as a result of this strategic planning effort? and, What results do we really want to achieve? need to be answered.

People who resist strategic planning often are those who have had "bad" experiences with it. Most bad strategic planning results from one or more of the following:

- lack of a defined scope
- poorly identified outcomes, goals, and objectives
- lack of prioritized goals
- lack of a tightly monitored timeline for delivery
- lack of maintenance.

This may require an examination of the current environment (to be discussed in more detail in later steps), or information may be available from customer surveys, market data, and other resources. However the information is acquired, planners must collect and analyze statistics and make a decisive effort to identify plan priorities. When the outcomes and priorities are identified, the goals and objectives of the plan can be established. This is a crucial component of the strategic planning process because the goals and objectives will determine where the effort should be concentrated and who needs to be involved. This also will affect the timetable and, ultimately, the tactics of the plan.

It is important to understand these two things: (1) strategic planning is not a reaction to the environment but an attempt to shape the future; and (2) using the information you have on hand will help determine priorities that will shape your entity into the organization, group, or department you want it to become. This effort will define the direction the organization will take generally, and the direction the departments and groups will take specifically. Ultimately, it will define what individual workers should do to make the company successful. A completed strategic plan frequently is the basis for funding, operational, or business planning, and for growth and management planning.

Planning Outcomes, Goals, and Objectives

Table 1.1 presents the outcomes, goals, and objectives for three organizations (financial services, health care, and technology) and

TABLE 1.1

Examples of Outcomes, Goals, and Objectives

Organization	Outcome	Goal	Objective	Group	Outcome	Goal	Objective
Financial services organization	To have a plan for a more profitable customer base	To reduce the cost per customer	To increase the number of relationships/ customers by more than 10 percent while ensuring that customer satisfaction remains the same	**Marketing department of the financial services organization**	To have a plan to support increasing customer relationships	To set up a marketing program aimed at increasing customer relationships	To establish new relationships with current customers and decrease the cost per customer by 15 percent in the first quarter
Health-care organization	To have a plan to meet nurses' union concerns	To decrease safety concerns for the nurses	To increase safety training that directly relates to injury claims by more than 50 percent	**HR department of the health-care organization**	To have a plan for safety training for the nurses	To develop a training program for nurse safety	By June, to launch a pilot program for nurse safety training that reduces injury claims by at least 50 percent

Technology organization	To have a plan that increases accountability for staying within budget	To increase cost/budget accuracy	To implement a new budget system to help managers increase cost/budget accuracy by 90 percent	Finance department of the tech organization	To have a plan to identify and implement a new system for budgeting	To increase cost/budget accuracy through a new budget tracking system	To increase cost/budget accuracy by 90 percent by providing managers with a new budget and reporting system, which will be tested and implemented before the next budgetary cycle

three departments within those organizations (marketing, HR, and finance). The purpose of this table is to show how outcomes, goals, and objectives help define the scope of a strategic plan.

You will see in table 1.1 that, in some cases, the link between the organization and the department responsible for executing the goals and objectives is very clear. In most instances, however, it will take several departments to accomplish the organizational goal. For example, in the financial services organization, the marketing department has responsibility for creating the marketing program; and in the health-care organization, the HR department will be responsible for developing new nurses' safety training. In this same table you also will note that the technology organization seeks a new budgetary system. This appears to be a finance department objective, but individual managers will have to be responsible and be held accountable for making sure the cost to budget is managed and decreased. Most likely, that will involve the information systems department developing specifications and determining both whether the company's existing equipment can support the new system and what systems will need to be linked to it (perhaps accounts payable and receivable).

The table illustrates the importance of linking department and group planning to the strategic plan and, ultimately, to individual performance plans. It's important to note that the objectives are measurable not only by percentage of change but also by a timetable commitment. Table 1.2 summarizes important criteria for setting strategic plan outcomes, goals, and objectives.

No more than 10 outcomes should be identified for a strategic plan. If you identify more than 10, take some time to compare them to your priorities. The outcomes should help you determine the roles and those accountable for defining the goals and objectives for the strategic plan's scope. To help you prioritize and decrease the number of outcomes you have identified, ask yourself the following four sets of questions:

1. How broad is the impact of this outcome? Will it affect the entire organization? What is the overall business im-

TABLE 1.2

Criteria for Plan Outcomes, Goals, and Objectives

Outcome Criteria	Goal Criteria	Objective Criteria
States what needs to be planned	Directly supports a stated strategic outcome	Is directly supportive of an outcome and goal
Projects the future of the organization	Is clear and lacks ambiguity or misinterpretation	Is measurable (by time, statistically, financially, or by other means) and can be verified
Includes key terms from which goals can be built	Aligns with the organization's values and culture	Is clear
Can be related to at least one goal	States a general intention, and needs not be measurable	Is something others within the organization can champion because they can relate to it
Makes writing a realistic plan possible	Is conceptual	Is tangible and concrete
Aligns with the organization's prioritized issues and needs	Is related to at least one (but preferably more) measurable objective(s)	Is consistent with the rest of the strategic plan
Describes something that will improve or provide a better future	Aligns with the organization's prioritized issues and needs	Aligns with the organization's prioritized issues and needs
Is consistent with the rest of the strategic plan's outcomes	• Has the support of senior management • Is realistic in its strategic intentions • Is feasible and can happen	• Is supported by senior management • Is realistic in its strategic intentions • Is feasible and can happen

pact? Will it improve the way we do business? Will it decrease quality problems or delays?

2. If we don't do this now, what will happen? Can this wait a couple of years? Will we lose market share, customers,

or employees? How big is the impact of not dealing with this now?

3. What is the financial impact of not addressing or fulfilling these outcomes, goals, and objectives now? Will it cost less to do it now than later? Is this an opportunity that will bring us a great deal of money? Is there a risk to the budget if this is not completed—a risk such as regulatory compliance, penalty, or fine?

4. Will it enrich or make employees' lives better and help the organization retain the "right" employees?

The sooner you identify the roles and accountabilities in the planning process, the better. If individuals and groups are involved early in the planning and have some say in preparation, they tend to be more committed. Creating and using a worksheet like the one illustrated in example 1.1 is helpful in assigning accountability for strategic planning.

In this example, B. Homez, senior manager of finance, is responsible for all of the outcomes. Because she is accountable for the results desired from the strategic plan, it is her responsibility to coordinate the other people responsible; to help them create outcomes, goals, and objectives; and to monitor their success to ensure the strategic outcome is met.

Determining the Timeframe

An important part of defining the scope for the strategic plan is determining the timeframe for developing the plan. This is a difficult task that depends on many factors, including

◆ *size of the organization:* Typically, the larger the organization, the more time it will take to create a strategic plan.

◆ *complexity of the organization:* If there are many departments, divisions, diverse product lines, varied customer groups, and lots of locations, the strategic plan will be more complex and will take longer to develop.

◆ *success rate of strategic planning:* If there is a successful strategic plan in place, it will take less time to create a re-

EXAMPLE 1.1

Financial Services Organization Example: Assigning Roles and Accountability

Group Represented	Outcome(s)	Senior Manager Accountable	Group or Department Responsible
Overall organization	To have a plan for a more profitable customer base	B. Homez	Branch/retail division
Marketing department	To have a plan to support increasing customer relationships	M. James	Marketing department
Customer services department	To have a plan to monitor and report on/react to the impact of the relationship-building campaign on customer satisfaction	D. Jamja	Customer relations group
Branch/retail division	To have a plan for a training and incentive program to increase relationship building	K. Li	Branch HR department
Finance department	To have a plan for monitoring the change in customer profitability relative to the new campaign	S. Duncan	Revenue group
Information technology department	To have a plan to create a system that will piggyback the new accounts systems to track the incentives and customer relationship to the account officer	R. Tucker	Information tech systems manager

vision. But if this is the first time a strategic plan is to be developed, it will take more time. Worse yet, if a plan has been created but never used, then it will take longer to gain commitment to plan development.

◆ *availability and accessibility of information* (such as employee satisfaction surveys, customer data, and financial data) needed for the planning effort: The rule is that the more data readily available, the shorter the timeframe for planning.

- *previous strategic planning experience in the organization:* It should take less time if those involved have experience in developing a successful strategic plan.
- *state of the business:* Is it stable or is it in turmoil? The more stable the business, the less time strategic planning will take.
- *resource availability:* For the plan to be written quickly, strategic planning needs to be a priority for those involved.
- *approval and signoff required:* The more channels involved in approving the strategic plan, the more time is needed. Completing the plan will take longer in a highly regulated or complex environment.

Generally speaking, small companies can produce a plan in less than three months, and most companies can launch a plan in six to 12 months. If a plan is already in place and just needs some maintenance, it can take fewer than 60 days to complete.

Identifying Key Participants

Key participants who will be involved as you develop the strategic plan include customers, stakeholders, and business partners. Another term used to identify these groups is *advocates.* These are the people who have a stake in the strategic plan and who will support its development and execution.

The term *customers* may refer to different parties for different objectives. For some objectives, the customer who uses the products and services is external to the organization; for others, he or she is within the organization.

Stakeholders are the people who have the most to gain from the business outcomes of the products and services offered by the organization. It is critical to identify stakeholders in the beginning of the strategic planning process because their support of the mission,

objectives, and plan will lend political strength. Committed stakeholders can help overcome barriers to gathering information, obtaining resources, and ensuring the success of the final plan.

Information for developing a strategic plan comes from a variety of sources, including

* external customers
* internal customers
* consultants
* research firms
* the competition
* business partners
* suppliers/vendors
* resellers
* stakeholders
* sponsors
* the public.

Business partners are those within or outside of the organization with whom you work to deliver your products and services, or those who have a similar stake in what you provide (for
example, Intel partners with hardware providers, such as HP,
IBM, and Dell, who use the computer chips Intel produces). They
are Intel customers *and* business partners because there is an end-
use customer who actually buys the computers. Another example
of a business partner relationship is a restaurant that partners with a soft drink company like Pepsi or
Coke. Although the restaurant is a customer of the soft drink com-
pany, they are business partners because they share the same end-
use customer, the diner. Multiple internal business partner relationships exist within organizations. Your department may be HR but
you are business partners with marketing, information systems, and
finance, and all of you must work together to achieve successful
outcomes.

Mapping Advocacy

A fourth key participant is a *sponsor*. If you are completing an internal strategy that fits under an organizationwide strategy, then
most likely you will have a sponsor. This is the executive or senior
manager who provides the financial approval for your group to
spend time and resources developing a plan. The sponsor may be
the department manager or someone else, depending on your orga-

nization's structure. The sponsor not only champions the development of the department strategic plan but also is responsible for ensuring that the completed plan is executed.

At this point, you should begin to have a feeling for how much information you have on hand and how much you will need to collect. You also should begin to know who would be a good member of the strategic planning work group. If you are a department or group that is developing a plan that is to guide your future work, then you need to ask yourself the following questions before proceeding:

- ◆ Is your department or group correctly aligned within the organization? Does the group report to a senior manager or to someone who reports to a senior manager who is directly involved in planning and implementing key initiatives within the organization? Does this senior manager understand the role the group plays in supporting and increasing the value of the organization?
- ◆ Does your group have the ability to identify the correct stakeholders for key initiatives and their customers, business partners, and sponsors? Does your group have access to those who hold key information so that you can gather the best information for key business decisions and plans?
- ◆ What do your advocates know about you?
- ◆ How do you interact with your advocates—is it in meetings, on a one-to-one basis, or via technology?
- ◆ What are the communication touch points? When do you communicate with your advocates?
- ◆ What is the structure of the organization (matrix, hierarchical, or some other form)? How does this structure affect advocacy?
- ◆ How are your customers' organizations structured and how does this affect your advocacy for the products and services that will best support them?

If your group is comfortable with the information it has about its advocates, you're ready to map your advocacy. Such mapping involves identifying your advocates and the benefits that accrue

POINTER

Resistance to change or new ideas is natural. Use the following techniques to overcome resistance to strategic planning:
- Ask questions.
- Explain the outcomes and benefits of strategic planning.
- Ensure the outcomes to be achieved by the plan are top priority for the organization.
- Clearly communicate the strategic planning process.
- Identify who owns the planning process and how others will be involved.
- Communicate what is and what is not known—and why this information is important to the future of the organization.
- Define the timeframe for plan development and let people know how you will use technology and other means to reduce development time.
- Address concerns on a one-to-one basis.

when there is a well-defined strategy. As you map advocacy for your plan, you clarify "what's in it for them" and how the strategy will support them. Mapping advocacy will help you

- identify, clarify, and validate for your advocates the benefits that will derive from developing a strategic plan
- determine if there is resistance to developing a plan, and if so, how to overcome it
- evaluate your presence as a strategic leader
- begin building an understanding of what it will take to gain commitment and support for the strategic plan to be executed.

Worksheet 1.1 can help you identify the benefits and strategic objectives for each advocate to be supported by the strategic plan. Examples of the four advocate types are provided to demonstrate how perspectives differ among advocates and how speaking to each perspective can be useful in gaining advocacy. If this worksheet is used in a group setting, be sure to address the additional facilitation questions provided in part B. The example given on the worksheet is of a planning and development group that delivers product training to internal customers.

WORKSHEET 1.1

Mapping Advocacy

Part A: Identifying Strategic Plan Advocates

Advocate Role	Defining Questions	Your Identified Advocate
Customer	• Who is the group or individual who pays for your programs? • Are there multiple funding methods? If so, who funds you, and how? • Who participates in your programs? • Do you have participants who are internal and external to your organization? • Do you have different levels of participants (for example, very technical, varied information needs, skill needs, knowledge-only needs)? ♦ Are there different levels of owners within your customer group (for example, business owner, team lead or supervisor, participant)? If so, what are the levels, and who represents each level? ♦ Who is the end-use customer? Are there different types of end-use customers (such as product-only buyers, product and service buyers)? ♦ Who relies on the implementation of skills or knowledge contained in your products and services to produce successful outcomes or end results back on the job?	
Stakeholder	• Who within your organization funds your products and services? • As a result of your products and services, who within your organization receives revenue?	

Business partner	◆ Who within your organization needs you to provide your products and services because they do not have the ability or time to do so? ◆ Who within your organization needs to partner with you because you provide their customers with the supporting products and services they need to be effective? ◆ Who do you need within your organization so that you can be effective? For example, who holds the information that you need to design your products and services? ◆ Who within your organization has information that you need about the customer? ◆ With whom inside your organization do you need to work so you can be effective?
Sponsor	◆ Who champions what you do within your organization? ◆ Who funds you within your organization? ◆ Who is committed to your existence within your organization?

Part B: Facilitation Questions

1. How does knowing your customers, stakeholders, business partners, and sponsors inform your strategic plan?

2. How will you use this information to move forward in building your strategic plan?

3. How will you validate this information?

4. Based on this discussion, what do you see differently regarding your customers, stakeholders, business partners, and sponsors, and how is this important to your planning process?

Gaining Commitment

Whether you are developing a strategic plan for the entire organization or one that is to guide a department or group, you will need to gain commitment to spend the time and resources needed to conduct the requisite research and develop the plan. If commitment is lacking, it usually means one of these three things:

1. The organization, department, or group isn't ready to start the process.
2. The benefits of strategic planning need to be better understood by the advocates.
3. Strategic planning was done in the past, was not done well, and did not guide or inspire the organization or group.

Regardless of the degree of commitment to develop a strategic plan within the organization, group, or department, you certainly will have to sell the plan to some or all of the players. It's helpful to start early by speaking with various participants who will bring or have input into the planning process, who know how to identify priorities, and who make the "big decisions." In strategic planning, as in many other things, people will react more positively if they understand what commitment they are being asked to make and what outcomes they may expect from that commitment. Tables 1.3 and 1.4 present tactics for overcoming resistance to strategic planning and the benefits of and selling points for developing a strategic plan.

At this point in Step 1 of the strategic planning process, you will either have the commitment needed to initiate plan development or you will need to meet with more advocates to strengthen their commitment. If you have strong relationships with your customers, stakeholders, business partners, and sponsors, you may need to do no more than let them know your intentions to develop and execute the plan. You also may find that you need additional resources from a particular party. If that's the case, worksheet 1.2 can help you identify additional advocates and the resources you lack. In column 1 of the worksheet, identify the role of any advocates from whom you

TABLE 1.3

Tactics for Overcoming Resistance to Strategic Planning

Type of Resistance	Tactic
Time: Developing a strategy takes a long time, with lots of meetings, and the advocate wants immediate action.	• Clarify how much time you think the process will take; then discuss the time requirements with your advocate. • Describe the negative consequences of not doing the strategy, including lost opportunities to save time and other costs. • Ask the advocate to help you identify ways to get to information or resources that will save time.
Too much data gathering: The advocate is concerned that your group is going after information that already exists.	• Ask for the advocate's assistance in identifying what information exists and where or how it can be obtained. Then map what information exists and what does not, and identify how best to collect the information that does not already exist. • Keep information gathering to a minimum, and gather only what is critical (this will be discussed further in Step 3). Demonstrate the leanness of your information gathering in a plan to collect data. • If possible, collect data from a central source, which is more efficient than collecting them from several sources.
Decision-making displacement (also known as politics): The advocate feels that, by developing and executing a group or department strategic plan, you will be making decisions that your business partners or stakeholders have authority to make.	• Be clear about what you want to know and why. • Demonstrate that you want to work with the advocate—not against him or her. • Demonstrate that you want the advocate's input, and stress the benefits of the plan for him or her. • Discuss the outcomes and results that will benefit the advocate if you develop and execute a strategic plan (for example, it will make her or him look good).

continued on next page

Table 1.3, continued

Type of Resistance	Tactic
Resource constraints: The advocate feels that there are only so many financial, human, and other resources, and that building a strategic plan might lessen her or his share.	• Discuss how a strategy will ensure that you manage resources more effectively. • Discuss the benefits of developing and executing a strategic plan. • Describe the negative resource consequences of not having the strategy. • Ask the advocate to help you identify ways to use resources more efficiently or effectively as part of your strategy definition.
Hidden agenda: You cannot ascertain the source of the resistance.	• Adopt a questioning mode. For example, ask, "How do you think we can be of better service? What is your vision of what we do? How can we serve your needs?" • Demonstrate that you want to work *with,* not against, the advocate. • If you don't gain the advocate's commitment in the first meeting, ask to meet for another discussion after you both have had time to think it through. Then review what was revealed during the intervening questioning period.
The advocate wants something other than a strategy: You're told, "Strategic planning is a waste; you should do...."	• Ask the advocate to describe what she or he thinks strategic planning is, and to reveal his or her vision of what you should do. • Discuss how both the strategic planning approach and the advocate's approach affect the business. • Discuss the process and goals of both approaches. • Discuss how both approaches address the people involved and the performance desired. • Discuss how both approaches address obstacles and barriers to achieving desired goals. • Determine if both of you are trying to get to the same place, but calling it different things. • Negotiate a common ground.

TABLE 1.4

Strategic Planning Benefits and Selling Points

Benefit	Selling Points
Strategic planning provides a structure or foundation for taking action.	• It sets goals that can be communicated and shared. • It creates a shared vision for all parties. • It provides a set of criteria and understandings for future decision making. • It establishes a timeframe for specific actions. • It identifies expected results or outcomes, and links those to business initiatives that will materialize as a result of action taken.
Strategic planning enables leadership to move forward.	• It creates energy for action. • It gives permission to move forward and make changes or initiate endeavors.
Strategic planning involves organizing data so that action can be taken.	• It provides information for informed decision making. • It provides a better understanding of the organization's environment. • It identifies current and potential trends. • It details the capabilities and limitations present in the organization. • It helps the organization, department, or group consider how it needs to respond to the future.
Strategic planning enables the organization, department, or group to manage its future.	• It provides an opportunity to review competitors' and others' actions and decide how the organization or unit will respond. • It helps identify what skills and knowledge the entity will need to be competitive. • It helps the organization, department, or group be proactive rather than reactive.
Strategic planning establishes a position.	• It illustrates where the organization, department, or group stands currently in the perspective of customers, competition, and others. • It creates a story of where the organization, department, or group is and where it has been. • It documents historical trends from organizational, departmental, or group history that can be used to address the future. • It identifies how the entity communicates, adapts to change, competes, and leverages its resources.

continued on next page

Table 1.4, continued

Benefit	Selling Points
Strategic planning creates a set of guidelines or rules for action.	• It identifies processes and procedures that are critical to the way the organization, department, or group does business. • It defines boundaries in allocating resources for opportunities that will provide results. • It identifies priorities for allocating resources and initiating action. • It identifies when the organization, department, or group should discontinue or update its programs or services.
Strategic planning makes the entity competitive.	• It makes the organization or unit more efficient and effective by promoting up-front planning. • It ensures that the entity has allocated and prioritized its resources effectively. • It provides criteria for evaluating actions, and ensures that the organization, department, or group is making wise decisions. • It orients the organization or unit thinking toward action rather than keeping it stuck in the past.
Strategic planning defines an organization's, department's, or group's value chain.	• It articulates key leverage points (areas where a small amount of resources yields a higher return). • It identifies the activities that add value to an entity's services and products, and the sequence in which those activities occur. • It describes why and how what the organization or unit does adds value.

still need commitment, and in column 2, list what you need them to provide. When you've identified whom and what you need, use part B to prompt a discussion of the *how*—how to gain commitment if the advocate and resource are not already on board. The worksheet provides a few examples to demonstrate its use.

Marketing Your Strategic Plan

After completing worksheet 1.2, you may have found you need to gather a great deal more information from your customers, stakeholders, business partners, and sponsors. If so, you must begin mar-

WORKSHEET 1.2

Identifying Additional Advocates and Resources

Part A: Gaining Commitment from Additional Advocates

Role of Advocate	What Advocate Must Commit to Provide	Is Advocate Committed?
Research and development	New product information for the next 12 months, including targeted customer demographics, product specifications, and product testing information	Yes ☐ No ☐
Customer call center	Data about customer requests and complaints, common customer questions	Yes ☐ No ☐
Sponsor (human resources manager)	Financial and time resources to engage in planning effort	Yes ☐ No ☐
		Yes ☐ No ☐
		Yes ☐ No ☐
		Yes ☐ No ☐
		Yes ☐ No ☐
		Yes ☐ No ☐

continued on next page

Part B: Facilitation Questions

1. Do we expect resistance from the advocates from whom we do not yet have commitment? If so, what type of resistance?

2. How will we overcome any resistance to developing and executing a strategic plan or to providing the information, resources, and so forth that we need to develop a plan?

3. Of the information needs listed above for which we do not have commitment, which is the most critical to the strategic plan?

4. Who will get the information—someone responsible for the strategic plan or the person in the resource role?

5. Who most likely would be successful in gaining the commitment, and why?

6. If we do not get the commitment needed, what is our back-up plan?

keting the idea of your plan to gain commitment from advocates and to collect the information needed to go forward. Even if you have all of the information you need, it's beneficial to hold group discussions about how to promote your efforts to build a strategic plan in routinely scheduled meetings, project meetings, or status reports. Informing others about what you're doing will encourage support and commitment, assuage concerns, and remove roadblocks.

You can use worksheet 1.3 to facilitate a group discussion to identify what you will communicate about your beginning work on the strategic plan. After you complete this worksheet, you will have an outline of what to communicate about the intent of the strategic plan and how you will develop it. You can build your presentation from this outline. Communication questions that your group should address are provided in the first column. In the second column, jot down your notes about the group's responses.

Tool 1.1 lists questions you can use to identify the tasks necessary for initiating the marketing for a strategic plan. This tool also can be used in a group discussion to identify who will be responsible for initiating these tasks and how they will do so.

WORKSHEET 1.3

Communicating Your Strategy

Communication Question	Your Notes
1. What is the purpose of the strategic plan?	
2. How do you intend to use the information you collected for the strategic plan?	
3. Why is there a need for the strategic plan in your organization's current environment?	
4. How will you communicate the status and results of the strategic plan on an ongoing basis?	
5. If someone needs more information about the strategic planning efforts, who within your group should he or she contact?	
6. Overall, how long do you expect the strategic plan development process to take, and what resources will you need?	

TOOL 1.1

Initiating and Evaluating Strategic Plan Marketing

Part A: The first part of this tool will help initiate the marketing for a strategic plan. It should be used in a group discussion that focuses on how to market the plan. Column 1 lists questions to help you identify the basic tasks you need to undertake in marketing the strategic plan to customers, business partners, management, employees, and possibly the public and/or press. Column 2 is provided for your notes about that task—your thoughts about why the task is important to your organization, the best methods for achieving it, the mechanisms already in place from which the task could be made less time consuming (for example, Websites or employee email blasts), and so on. In column 3, list the follow-up actions resulting from the discussion and identify a person who will lead each task. It's important that one person be identified who will be accountable for completing the task.

Questions for Brainstorming Marketing Tasks	Discussion Notes	Follow-up Action and Assigned Person
1. What is the status of the organization's strategic planning effort (past, present, future)?		
2. What are the reasons the organization is focusing on strategic planning now?		
3. What will be the key themes of the strategic plan?		
4. What is the message about the strategic plan you want presented to others?		
5. Are there different messages (one to customers, another to employees, to		

the public, to business partners, to management, and so forth)?	
6. What media are important to use to provide the message(s)?	
7. Is mixed media needed for one group or multiple groups (for example, an employee newsletter or email blast)?	
8. What is important about this initial planning for the strategic plan that you need to communicate to others?	
9. When should the strategic outcomes, goals, and objectives be communicated?	
10. To whom should the strategic outcomes, goals, and objectives be communicated?	
11. Who are our target audiences (now and in the future), and what behavioral changes do we want to see as a result of the strategic plan messages (for example, employees volunteer to be involved in the planning process)?	
12. Where have we been successful in conveying similar messages, and	

continued on next page

Tool 1.1, continued

Questions for Brainstorming Marketing Tasks	Discussion Notes	Follow-up Action and Assigned Person
why were we successful? Is that process transferable to this effort?		
13. How have other organizations like us successfully marketed their strategic plans? What could we learn from their experiences?		
14. How should the strategic outcomes, goals, and objectives be communicated?		
15. What resistance messages should be countered in the communication?		
16. How should the resistance messages be countered?		
17. What opportunities will the strategic plan provide that we as an organization aren't focusing on as we should?		
18. What communication vehicles are present today that should be used for communicating the strategic plan marketing, and to whom do they provide information?		
19. Who will need to review messages (legal department, strategic planning		

leadership, executive leadership, and so forth)?

20. What distribution strategy should be in place for this communication and for following communications about the strategy and its development?

21. Do we need some sort of promotional strategy (for example, free pizza at quarterly meetings held to talk about the strategy, free pencils with the mission)?

22. What is or will be our budget?

23. Who will be the contact if individuals want more information about the strategic plan?

24. Who will be the primary lead for the marketing of the strategic plan?

25. Who will take ownership/accountability for ensuring that the follow-up actions are completed by the people assigned and that the plan is implemented in a timely manner?

continued on next page

Tool 1.1, continued

Part B: Here is a list of questions to help you evaluate the effectiveness of the marketing tasks and their results. The questions are listed in column 1 and space is provided in column 2 for your discussion notes.

Questions for Evaluating the Strategic Plan Marketing	Discussion Notes
1. Are/were the leadership roles and accountabilities defined, and did the people assigned follow through? How do you know?	
2. The purpose of the marketing is not to convey a message, but to change behaviors and thoughts. Was this successful? How? What is the evidence?	
3. Did those involved in reviewing the strategic planning efforts provide timely feedback and assistance?	
4. Did a two-way communication occur between the strategic planners and others as a result of the marketing effort?	

5. Was interest in the strategic plan evident in the audiences? How? Was this positive for the development of the plan?

6. Did the promotion tactics work? Why or why not, and how?

7. Did the media used meet the audiences' needs? How do you know?

8. Was communication about the strategic planning efforts consistent and regular?

9. Were the messages influential?

10. Were the messages credible?

11. Were the communication methods creative, and did they capture the audiences' attention? How do you know?

◆ ◆ ◆

Now it's time to turn your attention to Step 2 of strategic planning. In that step you'll begin to involve others in developing the plan. The next step focuses on conducting a kickoff meeting and identifying the data that need to be collected to validate the outcomes, goals, and objectives drafted in Step 1.

NOTES

_____

_____

_____

_____

_____

_____

_____

_____

_____

_____

_____

_____

_____

_____

_____

_____

_____

Scanning the Business Environment

Scanning the business environment is the work of the second step in strategic planning. The information gathered during this step will help you decide if the outcomes, goals, and objectives you identified in Step 1 are the right priorities for the organization or unit to pursue. Analyzing what you discover will not only validate if they are correct, but also will tell you if any modifications are needed. This step is enormously important in defining the focus of the strategic plan.

During Step 2, you will research issues your organization faces today and will face in the future. To accomplish this you must find out about the organization's current status, its history, development, and growth. Examining the past as well as the present will help you understand why the organization functions the way it does today and will help point out gaps or needs that were missed previously. By scanning your business environment you also gain a better understanding of the organization's strengths, weaknesses, opportunities, and threats (SWOT).

POINTER

As a champion of the strategic plan, if you want to be effective you must be clear about the direction your organization is moving and about what and how your department's or group's programs, services, and products address the organization's future needs.

What you scan in the business environment depends on where the organization and industry are in their life cycles. For example, the organization may be young and in a growth cycle. Or perhaps it is an older, more established company within a mature industry in "shakeout mode"—where only the strongest and most agile will survive. Maybe the organization is at a declining point in its life cycle and needs to institute significant change to maintain viability.

Another aspect of scanning the business environment is identifying the business drivers that are affecting the organization today. Identifying these drivers requires answering questions such as, Is the economy slowing? Has a natural disaster occurred that has depleted critical resources? Are there new developments in technology that are reshaping how a certain piece of business is done?

You champion the strategic plan; and if you want to be effective in that effort, you must be clear about the direction your organization is moving and about what and how your department's or group's programs, services, and products address the organization's future needs. You have to be able to explain your group's role in building a sustainable competitive advantage and the ways you will partner with line functions to assess and address corporate needs. The best way to begin this step of the process is to put together a strategic planning work group that comprises key players who can help you scan the environment and make pivotal business decisions for the organization, department, or group.

In this step of the strategic plan development process, we'll address the following topics:

- ◆ kicking off strategic plan development
- ◆ building the project plan for strategy development
- ◆ collecting business information

- conducting a SWOT analysis
- identifying your organization's business drivers
- crafting questions to use in interviews with executives
- setting guidelines for data collection.

Case Examples: Scanning the Environment

Step 2 provides an opportunity to draw others into the strategic planning process by involving them in scanning the business and by assigning roles and accountabilities for supporting this activity and developing the strategic plan. The principal activities in this step are illustrated in the following two examples.

Dealing With a Wealth of Information

Com-Uni-Kate is a relatively new communications firm with fewer than 25 employees. Leadership believes the organization would benefit greatly from developing a strategic plan to guide its efforts and growth for the next 36–48 months. The strategic planning committee is overwhelmed with the amount of industry information it has gathered from external sources during the business scanning step. It's unsure how or if it should use all this material, and how or if the data relate to the previously identified strategic outcomes, goals, and objectives. And if the data don't relate, the committee wonders what action, if any, the organization should take. The committee wants to use SWOT analysis to identify missing information that will help the organization close its gaps and maximize its strengths and opportunities.

Using Careful Planning to Sustain Growth

Tucker Enterprises is a company that went public a little less than a year ago, and strong sales and soaring stock prices have made the organization flush with cash. It has identified four key outcomes for its strategic plan:

1. Identify solid opportunities to invest cash and continue growth.
2. Identify ways to sustain competitive advantage in a new and fast-growth industry.
3. Manage rapid growth.
4. Create a sound financial strategy.

Although Tucker Enterprises feels comfortable with these four outcomes, it wants to ensure that the goals and objectives defined are complete and that nothing is missing in its strategy. The company wants to validate these outcomes (and their corresponding goals and objectives) during its analysis of the business environment. The strategy work group has come together to identify any other data that need to be collected and what, if any, contrary data exist.

Kicking Off Strategic Plan Development

When you've clarified the benefits of strategic planning; identified draft outcomes, goals, and objectives; and decided how you will sell the development of the plan, you're ready to kick off the development cycle. You know you can't develop a strategy in eight hours, but you can hold a one-day kickoff meeting—preferably off site. This meeting gives everyone a chance to get on the same page and commit to the work ahead.

Any resistance to the strategic plan should have been addressed before the kickoff meeting, but if any arises there, it's wise to address it before moving on. Tool 2.1 is an example of an agenda for this meeting.

To ensure this meeting is productive and stays on track, it's helpful to set a few meeting rules. Tool 2.2 lists guidelines for a kickoff meeting. Send a copy of this tool (customized to fit your corporate culture) and the meeting agenda to all participants so everyone understands the meeting guidelines and topics to be covered. It may be helpful to enlarge and post these guidelines in the meeting room and refer to them as needed.

TOOL 2.1

Sample Agenda: Strategic Planning Kickoff Meeting

Date: _____

Meeting Objectives

* To present the benefits of strategic planning for our organization *(information provided in Step 1)*
* To present the drafts of the outcomes, goals, and objectives, as we know them to be at this point *(information provided in Step 1)*
* To identify what data need to be collected *(information provided in Step 2)*
* To assign roles and responsibilities for data collection to specific people *(information provided in Step 2)*
* To identify a timeline for data collection and reporting *(information provided in Step 2)*

Agenda

7:30 a.m.	Gathering time—coffee, tea, and water provided
7:45 a.m.	Introductions, a review of meeting objectives and guidelines, and discussion of how the meeting will be conducted
8:00 a.m.	Benefits of strategic planning presented
8:15 a.m.	Drafts of outcomes, goals, and objectives presented, and short explanation about how they were identified
8:45 a.m.	Presentation of currently available information (company history, employee satisfaction survey data, customer product satisfaction data, and competitive analysis)
9:45 a.m.	Break
10:00 a.m.	Discussion of the organization's strengths, weaknesses, opportunities, and threats
11:30 a.m.	Presentation, discussion, and brainstorming on the information that remains to be collected prior to developing the strategic plan
12:30 p.m.	Working lunch, with discussion of and brainstorming about the organization's business drivers—past, present, and future
1:45 p.m.	Review of information to be collected (any additions following the afternoon discussions)
2:30 p.m.	Discussion of and brainstorming about the data analysis process
3:15 p.m.	Break
3:30 p.m.	Assignment of roles and accountabilities for data collection
4:15 p.m.	Discussion of the timeline for data reporting and meeting to discuss results
4:45 p.m.	Open discussion and wrap-up

TOOL 2.2

Guidelines for the Strategic Planning Kickoff Meeting

These guidelines have been established for the strategic plan development kickoff meeting to be held on [date]. Your cooperation in following these guidelines is appreciated.

1. Arrive on time and be prepared for this meeting.

2. Assign someone to handle important calls and emails for you while you are in the meeting. We ask that you be contacted only in an emergency. (The emergency contact number is [fill in].)

3. There will be opportunities for discussion, but because our time is limited, any discussions other than those on the agenda will be tabled until a later time.

4. The drafts of the strategic plan outcomes, goals, and objectives will be presented in this meeting. However, we won't spend time discussing them. Any discussion of these will be postponed until after critical data have been collected.

5. If you have organizational information, such as customer satisfaction data, employee data, financial data, company history, or any other information you think is pertinent to developing the strategic plan, please forward a copy to [contact name] before [date].

6. If you are assigned the responsibility of collecting certain information, you may delegate this to another person—but you ultimately are accountable for this information's timely gathering and reporting.

7. The final deadline for data gathering and reporting has been set for [date]. If any data you think are crucial to the development of the strategic plan will not be available until after that date, please contact [name] immediately. Bringing it up in the meeting is not acceptable.

8. Review the attached agenda and, if you have any questions or suggestions, contact [name] by [date].

We appreciate your attendance and cooperation. You're an important member of the Strategic Planning Group!

Thank you.

[name]

When you customize the guidelines, it's important to gain senior management's approval of them. Doing so begins the top-down initiation of the plan development process, and it will help overcome resistance that could come to the surface during the kickoff meeting.

Building the Project Plan for Strategy Development

Another aim of the initial meeting is to begin to build the *project plan* for developing the strategic plan. The project plan defines the tasks that strategic planning requires and establishes a schedule for their completion. Introducing at least an outline of the project plan at this early point in your overall strategy development helps everyone involved. Estimating the time the various strategic planning tasks will take is an art. The timing of these tasks depends on the type and size of your organization and on its previous experience with strategic planning, among other things. You may find commercially available project planning software helpful in setting up and maintaining your project plan—and your organization probably has this software in-house.

Table 2.1 will help you think about strategic planning time requirements in the context of our 10-step strategic plan development process. Column 1 lists the 10 steps to strategic planning and the organization-specific factors that either shorten or lengthen the time needed to develop the strategic plan. The remaining three columns suggest the amounts of time you'll need for each step, depending on how much effort your organization will have to expend to accomplish it—that is, the *impact* that completing the step will have on your organization. For example, let's say the planning group already has mounds of business environment data in hand, but the organization has no mission statement. Completing Step 2's scanning will take the least time (that is, have minimal impact on the organization), but preparing a mission statement from scratch in Step 5 will likely take most of the time allotted (and so have maximal impact).

Collecting Business Information

An important part of strategic plan development is knowing what information to collect. The business information needed for developing a sound plan includes, but is not limited to, the following items:

TABLE 2.1

Using the 10-Step Process to Forecast Your Project Plan Schedule

Strategy Planning Step and Factors Affecting Its Impact on the Organization	Time Required, Minimal Impact	Time Required, Moderate Impact	Time Required, Maximal Impact
Step 1: Laying the foundation • Amount of information available • Previously identified and met outcomes, goals, and objectives • Existent marketing plan and communication vehicles • Identification of advocates • Size of the organization	2–3 weeks	30–60 days	60–90 days
Step 2: Scanning the business environment • Amount of information available • Amount of information mapping completed • Identification of past and present business drivers • Level of support for additional data collection (survey builder, technology, resources, funds, and so forth) inside the organization • Size of the organization	30–60 days	60–90 days	3–4 months
Step 3: Collecting relevant data • Amount of information available • Availability of internal trained resource to collect and validate data • Resistance of data sources to providing necessary information • Size of the organization	10–20 days	20–45 days	45–90 days

Step (factors)			
Step 4: Analyzing collected data • Amount of information available • Availability of internal trained resource to code and sort data • Amount of data validated • Availability of technology to support data analysis • Size of the organization	2–3 weeks	3–5 weeks	5–8 weeks
Step 5: Stating mission, vision, and values • Existence of a mission statement • Existence of a list of organizational objectives • Degree to which the organization consistently gives clear mission-appropriate messages to customers, employees, and others	1–3 days	1–5 days	1–10 days
Step 6: Prioritizing business needs and identifying risks • Amount of information available • Consistency and validity of data provided • Number of hidden agendas within the organization • Commitment or resistance to the strategy's mission, outcomes, goals, and objectives • Need for debate and/or consensus concerning the organization culture • Size of the organization	1–3 weeks	2–4 weeks	2–6 weeks
Step 7: Designing and validating tactics • Amount of information available • Consistency and validity of data provided • Need for debate and/or consensus concerning the organization culture • Early agreement on original outcomes, goals, and objectives	1–2 weeks	2–3 weeks	2–6 weeks

continued on next page

STEP
2

Table 2.1, continued

Strategy Planning Step and Factors Affecting Its Impact on the Organization	Time Required, Minimal Impact	Time Required, Moderate Impact	Time Required, Maximal Impact
◆ Experience with developing plans and tactics ◆ Size of the organization			
Step 8: Prioritizing tactics and resources ◆ Amount of information available ◆ Consistency and validity of data provided ◆ Organization culture (the impact of resource allocation on pay, benefits, and so forth) ◆ Amount of competition for resources within the organization ◆ Number of hidden agendas ◆ Early agreement to original outcomes, goals, and objectives ◆ Amount of experience in prioritizing resources ◆ Size of the organization	1–2 weeks	2–3 weeks	2–5 weeks
Step 9: Documenting and communicating the plan ◆ Existence of previous plan or outline ◆ Experience with strategic planning and documentation ◆ Existence of marketing plan and communication vehicles for this type of project ◆ Size of the organization	3–5 days	7–10 days	2–3 weeks
Step 10: Maintaining the plan ◆ Existence of maintenance plan for previous strategic plan ◆ Agreement about triggers for maintenance ◆ Volatility of the environment ◆ Size of the organization	1 day	1–2 days	1–2 days

◆ *benchmarking data:* identifying the best practices in various areas and applying those to your own organization

◆ *investment climate assessment:* "testing the waters," particularly when looking at other countries in which to invest or locate operations or when expanding product lines

◆ *survey data:* pinpointing one or more specific population sets and asking specific questions

◆ *focus group or blog gathering:* using face-to-face or technology-to-technology methods to gather qualitative information about specific subjects

◆ *SWOT assessment:* looking at the organization's present and future directions

◆ *history:* reviewing the data that explain not only the time-line but also what happened to the organization as it developed and grew over time; investigating what the growth trends mean to today's organization and to its future

◆ *today's organizational structure:* reviewing the current structure and its control system, and discovering how it supports or detracts from the strategy to be pursued

◆ *external environment:* identifying the environmental and competitive threats; discovering whether there is a potential environmental problem or a problem with the source of a product; evaluating how the competition is doing and if any competitor has become a market-share "piranha"

◆ *financial analysis:* determining the organization's financial status; evaluating how the organization's financial ratios compare with others of its size and in its sector

◆ *public perception:* identifying how the public views the organization (as a community player; as a contributor to or a detractor from the community at large)

◆ *customer perception:* identifying how customers feel about the organization and its products, services, and processes; defining the relationship between the organization and its customer base

◆ *employee perception:* learning how employees feel about the organization and its products and services, and its work and business processes; defining the relationship between the organization and its employees.

It's obvious that you can collect a massive amount of information while scanning the business environment. But some of it isn't needed for strategic planning purposes. To ensure your scan of the business environment isn't a bloated and futile exercise, focus on gathering material related to the strategic plan's outcomes, goals, and objectives. Table 2.2 lists various strategic plan outcomes and the information needed to formulate a strategy for accomplishing those outcomes. Tool 2.3 is a mapping tool that shows how using the outcomes, goals, and objectives you have identified for the organization can help you focus and make the most of your information collection efforts.

As a result of your environment scanning, you may have identified new outcomes or reprioritized those previously discussed. Remember that, as you develop the strategic plan, you are in a state of "work and discovery," so the plan will change as you move through the 10 steps, and the plan that emerges at the end will provide the benefits you identified earlier in the planning process and will guide your organization into its desired future.

Prior to the kickoff meeting, it may be helpful to use Tool 2.3 to identify as many current information sources as possible and then to use the tool to present those sources at the meeting. Additional information sources may be identified by other attendees and the tool can be updated accordingly. Using the same tool with the updated information, brainstorm to identify what information remains to be collected, the potential sources for that information, who might be able to obtain the information, and who ultimately is responsible for gathering it.

The information you need to collect depends on the direction or scope of your strategic plan. Table 2.3 lists the types of information most frequently needed for strategic planning and suggests possible sources of that information.

Although Table 2.3 lists information sources directly related to customer information, it is important to stress that just because

TABLE 2.2

Information Needed to Secure Different Outcomes

Outcome	Information Needed
To expand product line into different markets nationally and internationally	◆ What type of markets does the product fit into? ◆ What are the methods for market expansion? ◆ What global perspectives do we need to understand? ◆ What sector-level studies do we need to conduct? ◆ What country-level information and benchmarking data do we need? ◆ What business regulations might affect marketing and selling our product(s) in other markets? ◆ What are the economic forecasts for other markets?
To deepen customer relationships with the organization	◆ What is our current customer satisfaction rating? ◆ What methods do other companies use to deepen customer relationships? ◆ What is the competition doing to deepen customer relationships? ◆ Are there customer segments or types of customers we want to target first? Why and how?
To reduce time to market	◆ What is involved in getting to market? ◆ For which products is it most necessary to reduce time to market? ◆ What are other companies doing to reduce time to market? ◆ What is the competition doing to reduce time to market? ◆ What will it mean in savings and cost to reduce time to market?
To improve quality and reduce errors in new development	◆ What are our current quality and error rates in new development? ◆ What are the costs (employee, product, customer, production) associated with errors? ◆ Are quality and errors training issues? ◆ What are the quality and error rates in other organizations that create a similar product?

continued on next page

Table 2.2, continued

Outcome	Information Needed
	◆ What are the competition's quality and error rates? ◆ Is this a business process issue?
To decrease costs per employee	◆ What is the current cost per employee? ◆ In what area do we spend the most on employees today? ◆ In what area do we spend the least on employees today? ◆ Why are (or what makes) employee costs what they are today (for example, past promises, rise in outside costs)? ◆ What type of issues might arise if we change the environment for employees by reducing costs (such as union issues, turnover, employee dissatisfaction)? ◆ What are other companies doing to reduce costs per employee? ◆ What is the competition doing to reduce costs per employee?
To strengthen the bench of potential managers	◆ What is the bench today? ◆ What are the key competencies that need to be strengthened for the bench? ◆ Which current employees are considered bench potential today? ◆ Do those employees have the appropriate competencies and criteria? ◆ Where are we most likely to need new senior leaders in the future? ◆ Do we have bench trained for those roles? ◆ How do others create a strong bench in their organizations? ◆ How does the competition create a strong bench?
To decrease employee turnover and increase retention rates	◆ Why do employees leave? ◆ Does retention vary by department? If so, why? ◆ What is the cost of each employee turnover? ◆ What methods do other organizations use to retain employees? ◆ Is the competition facing the same issue? ◆ What is the impact of turnover on customers, on public perception of the organization, on new employee recruitment, and on business processes?

TOOL 2.3

Information Mapping Tool

Outcome	Goal	Objective	Type of Information Needed	Information Source/Location
To have a plan for a more profitable customer base	To reduce the cost per customer	To increase the number of relationships/customers by more than 10 percent while ensuring customer satisfaction remains the same	• Customer segmentation • Customer satisfaction data • Product or service relationships per customer	• Marketing department • No known data • Customer information system
To have a plan to identify and implement a new system for budgeting	To increase cost/budget accuracy through a new budget tracking system	To increase by 90 percent the accuracy of cost/budget by providing managers with a new budget and reporting system, which will be tested and implemented prior to the next budgetary cycle	• Departmental budget/cost information • Department managers' budget reporting needs • Cost of new system • Current reports available from previous system	• Finance department • No known data • Finance department • Finance department
To strengthen the current potential management bench	To ensure there are new senior leaders available on the bench	To identify the competencies needed for the bench and to ensure at least two or three potential managers are ready for each potential leadership position	• Content of the bench today • Key competencies that need to be strengthened for the bench • Degree to which employees have the appropriate competencies and criteria	• HR department • Unknown • Unknown

continued on next page

STEP

2

51

Tool 2.3, continued

Outcome	Goal	Objective	Type of Information Needed	Information Source/Location

TABLE 2.3

Information Needed and Potential Sources

Type of Information	Examples of Information	Potential Sources
Employee data	• Employee satisfaction • Available training • Retention, cost per employee, and other statistics • Benchmarking	• Surveys • HR department • HR information system • American Society for Training & Development (www.astd.org) • Society for Human Resource Management (www.shrm.org) • U.S. Bureau of Labor Statistics (www.bls.gov)
Global market information	• Economic information • Regulatory costs • Country reports	• World Bank Group (www.worldbank.org, www.ifc.org, www.doingbusiness.org) • U.S. government reports (https:www.cia.gov/cia/publications/factbook/index/html) • World Advertising Research Center (www.warc.com)
Industry information	• Industry climate • Regulation • Enterprise information	• U.S. government publications and Websites • Dun and Bradstreet (and subsidiaries) • Global Insights (www.global.insight.com)
Organization history	• Historical financial data • Historical market data • Historical customer data • Historical product data	• Prior annual reports • Prior business plans and cases • New employee orientation handouts and videos • American Historical Association (www.historians.org)
Customer data	• Customer satisfaction data • Customer complaints • Costs per customer • Products per customer	• Customer information system • Finance department • Marketing department • Call center or customer support department • Sales and marketing workforce • Business Chambers Website search engine (www.businesschambers.com)

continued on next page

Table 2.3, continued

Type of Information	Examples of Information	Potential Sources
Marketing and sales data	• Marketing campaign • Product segmentation • Cost per product • Product/service time to market • Customer segmentation	• Marketing department • Finance department • Research/development and design department • Manufacturing department • American Association of Advertising Agencies (www.aaaa.org) • Public Relations Society of America (www.prsa.org)
Financial information	• Cost data • Profit ratios • Liquidity ratios • Activity ratios • Leverage ratios • Shareholder ratios • Return-on-investment information	• Finance department • Business finance reports • Annual report and business plan • Finance system • Business news services (www.reuters.com; www.bloomberg.com, www.barrons.com)
Business processes information	• Current process steps and outcomes • Process documentation	• Process owner • Employees engaging in the process • Training guides • Business Process Management Initiative (www.bpmi.org) • Object Management Group (www.omg.org)
Quality control data	• Quality statistics • Number of errors • Quantity of scrap • Accidents and injuries	• Incident reports • Quality system reports • Those accountable for quality • Statsoft, Inc. (www.statsoft.com)
Research and development data	• Plans for release • Problems in testing	• Prereleased organizational communication pieces • Digital communication • Testing results • *R&D* magazine (www.rdmag.com) • Virtual Salt (www.virtualsalt.com/evaluat8it.htm) • Community Research and Development Information Service (www.cordis.lu) • American Chemical Society (www.pubs.acs.org)

your organization has identified a customer outcome, you shouldn't look only at customer and product data. Identify other factors that will be affected by that outcome, such as

- *employees:* For example, if the way employees are paid will change, the effect of this change on job satisfaction levels becomes important if you don't want to increase turnover costs. If a training program is part of the solution for achieving a desired outcome, then costs, time, and metrics need to be identified to ensure that training is successful.

- *financial aspects:* It is important to explore the costs and benefits associated with the tactics you plan to use to reach the desired outcomes, but first you have to identify and understand the financial reasons for this outcome.

- *perception:* It's important to learn how the public, the competition, and your customers themselves perceive what it is you're trying to accomplish.

- *business processes:* Most outcomes require that business processes change. Understanding the current processes before making changes is crucial to future success. Without fully understanding a process and how it may interact with other processes, you cannot ask customers the right questions or understand the full effect of changing the process.

While gathering data for an outcome, it's important to focus on more than one component and to think of what else will be affected. The strategic planning group often identifies missing or contrary information that should be collected. For example, gathering useful financial indicators frequently is left out of the strategic planning business scan. This may result from the mistaken notion that such indicators aren't germane if the outcomes are focused on customer satisfaction, new markets, or altered business processes. Table 2.4 lists some of the key financial indicator categories that might be helpful to review. Consider having a discussion with your company's financial leader to identify those financial indicators that are particularly important to your organization.

Financial indicator information should be looked at from several perspectives. Be sure to do the following:

TABLE 2.4

Helpful Financial Indicators for Business Analysis

Financial Indicator Category	Types of Ratios Provided and Formula to Discover It	Why the Indicator Is Important
Profit ratios	◆ Gross profit margin: (Sales revenue – Cost of goods sold) / Sales revenue ◆ Net profit margin: Net income / Sales revenue ◆ Return on total assets is a percentage of net income available to common shareholders' total assets ◆ Return on shareholder equity is a percentage of net income available to common shareholders' equity	Profit ratios measure the ability of the organization to use its resources efficiently. A helpful method to use in developing your organization's strategy is to compare the organization's ratios against those of its competitors. That tells you if you are more or less efficient and cost effective than the competition.
Liquidity ratios	◆ Current ratio: Current assets / Current liabilities ◆ Quick ratio: (Current assets – Inventory) / Current liabilities	Liquidity ratios measure the organization's ability to liquefy its assets to cover debts. (Liquid assets are usually cash, accounts receivable, and so forth.) The higher the liquidity ratio, the more likely there is funding capacity for research.
Activity ratios	◆ Inventory turnover: Cost of goods sold / Inventory ◆ Average collection period: Accounts receivable / (Total sales / 360)	Activity ratios are indicators of the ability of the organization to manage assets. If the activity ratios are below competition, a new outcome may be needed. Organizations need to demonstrate to creditors and shareholders that they are effective in managing their assets.

| Leverage ratios | ◆ Debt-to-assets ratio: Total debt / Total assets
◆ Debt-to-equity ratio: Total debt / Total equity
◆ Times covered ratio: Profit before interest and tax / Total interest charges | If an organization uses more debt than equity, it is "highly leveraged." The balance between debt and equity is called *capital structure*. An organization wants debt to be at the lowest cost possible. However, any debt is risky because enough profit must be made to cover both the original debt (or principal) and the resulting interest owed. Often a strategy will be to lower the debt-to-assets ratio or the times covered ratio. This ultimately lowers the cost of the debt (and risk) to the organization. |
| Shareholder return ratios | ◆ Price-to-earnings ratio: Market price per share / Earnings per share
◆ Market-to-book value: Market price per share / Earnings per share
◆ Dividend yield: Dividend per share / Market price per share | These ratios may not apply to your organization if the company is young or in the earlier stages of its life cycle and if dividends are not paid out. An organization also may not pay out dividends if the funds need to go to research and development. But to retain shareholders (and the debt and support they provide), the organization must provide a competitive return on shareholder investment. |

- Compare the indicators to the competition, the industry, and benchmarks for successful organizations. This may identify other outcomes that should be priorities for the strategic plan.
- Compare the indicators to past indicators for your organization or to financial trends for your organization. If you see an increase in debt-to-assets ratio, it may not be a good time to invest in a campaign that is rich in costs and slow to turn into revenue.
- Analyze the outcomes you have identified against the most important financial indicators to identify meaningful financial metrics for those outcomes.

Conducting a SWOT Analysis

SWOT analysis identifies the organization's strengths (for example, competitive advantage, strong brand, good locations, strong training programs for new managers), weaknesses (such as poor employee morale, start-up cash drain, cash-flow problems, public reputation), opportunities (like a new product line, technology, research, communication structure, employee benefits structure), and threats (such as the economy, weather or natural disasters, legislative regulation, the leadership bench). Worksheet 2.1 can be used as a tool to conduct this type of audit for the current organization and to identify existing gaps when comparing the results to the organization's future.

It may be helpful to follow these guidelines when completing the SWOT analysis worksheet from the organizational view:

1. Be realistic.
2. Don't over-think or over-analyze—just say what first comes to mind.
3. Think "organization today and where it should be tomorrow"—don't dwell on the past.
4. Recognize that SWOT is subjective and that you may need additional data to support your findings.

WORKSHEET 2.1

SWOT Analysis Worksheet

Instructions: Describe your organization's strengths, weaknesses, opportunities, and threats relative to the factors affecting the organization.

Key Factor	Strengths	Weaknesses	Opportunities	Threats
Competition				
Political effects				
Regulation				
Market developments				
Research				
Innovation				
Communication				
Economy				
Technology				

continued on next page

STEP 2

Worksheet 2.1, continued

Key Factor	Strengths	Weaknesses	Opportunities	Threats
Human resources				
Marketing				
Finance				
Revenue streams				
Costs				
Cash flow				
Core activities				
Accreditations/certifications				
Continuity, supply chain robustness				
Succession, bench				
Benefits/salary				
Global markets				

Price, value, quality			
Customer base			
Customer service			
Business partners			
Market demand			
Brand			
Public perception/reputation			
Key staff			
Training			
New employees			
Project management			
Niche target markets/core markets/products			

continued on next page

Worksheet 2.1, continued

Key Factor	Strengths	Weaknesses	Opportunities	Threats
Organization culture				
Experience, knowledge, data				
Communication/Information flows				
Management of strategic change				
Control systems				
Goodwill				
Portfolio management				
Investments				
Other considerations unique to your organization:				

When you've completed the business scan of the organization and identified the strengths, weaknesses, opportunities, and threats that exist now, use the worksheet again. Review each of the desired outcomes in your strategic plan, paying attention to how the outcomes will affect the future of the organization. For example, if a desired outcome is to build a new customer information system to increase sales with current customers, a SWOT analysis will help you determine the organization's strengths and abilities to complete the development, its weaknesses in doing so, the opportunities that will come from the new system, and the threats involved in developing or not developing the system.

When you've completed both audits (of the organization as a whole and of the strategic plan outcomes), compare the two worksheets and ask the following questions:

1. How will the outcomes help our organization move toward the desired future?
2. How will the outcomes hinder our organization in moving toward the desired future?
3. What else needs to happen in our organization to move it toward the desired future, and is this of a higher priority than any of our desired outcomes?

Identifying Business Drivers

The next activity in Step 2 is a critical step in creating a strategic plan—identifying the organization's business drivers—situations that prompt an organization to take specific actions. Both external and internal factors create business drivers (and you may have noted their effects during the SWOT analysis).

External business drivers usually are outside of an organization's control. Here are some examples:

♦ *economic drivers:* upturns or downturns in the economy, embargoes or trade restrictions, other situations prompted by the national or international economy

- *human resource drivers:* shortages of resources or of certain skills, union demands or contracts, employee needs to balance family and work relationships
- *government drivers:* regulation or deregulation that forces changes in competition or the environment as a whole
- *public perception drivers:* the public's view of the organization, sometimes influenced by press coverage of an event or situation outside the organization's control
- *market or customer drivers:* changes in customer demographics, definition, and needs that place demands on products or change product design; increased competition; other changes in how the organization views the marketplace in which it competes.

An example of an external driver affecting business today is the increased cost of fuel. This driver is forcing a change in product design, manufacture, and shipping, and in a host of business processes and policies.

Internal business drivers are generated by factors and events within the organization's control, although an internal driver may be a response to an external driver. Typically, there is a stakeholder inside the organization for this type of driver, an important consideration in creating a performance improvement strategy. Internal business drivers include

- *technology drivers:* innovations and new technology that create opportunities or needs for changes in the way information is kept, processed, and exchanged
- *process, system, or key policy drivers:* changes in work processes, systems, or key policies that change employee skill or behavior requirements

POINTER

The cost of gasoline is an *external* driver in today's business world. This driver, which is outside the control of the organization, forces changes in product design, location of manufacture, and shipping methods, among other things. Travel costs of all kinds force changes in business processes and policies.

An example of an *internal* driver is the organization's installing a new computer-based performance management system. Having this tool creates a need for new procedures, training, and possibly salary guideline changes.

- *shareholder or financial drivers:* responses to investor or bank demands for higher profits or lower costs reflected on the balance sheet
- *leadership or organization drivers:* reorganizations or leadership changes that prompt other changes; a cultural shift typically occurs that brings the organization into alignment with the values and perspective of the new leadership.

An example of an internal driver is the installation of a new computer-based performance management system. Using the system means devising new procedures, training, and possibly changes in salary structure.

Identifying the business drivers for your organization, for your customers (and their corresponding performance needs), for the group or department, and for the business partners of the group or department is the foundation for answering the following questions:

- Where do shared business alliances exist?
- Where do differences in businesses lie, and how critical are they to each business? What impact will these differences have on your organization's strategic plan?
- How can you effectively and efficiently help your customers and business partners respond to their business drivers while responding appropriately to your own?

Worksheet 2.2 will help you identify the business drivers for the organization, your customers, your business partners, and your own group. The facilitation questions in part B help you discuss how the alignment of the business drivers (or the lack of it) will affect the development and execution of your strategy. There are examples in the worksheet that illustrate its use.

Crafting Executive Interview Questions

Although it is important to have the organization's executives in alignment early on in the development of a strategic plan, it's also useful to get their individual feedback about the organization at this point in the process. Each key executive should have been con-

WORKSHEET 2.2

Identifying Business Drivers

Part A

	Organization Drivers	Customer Drivers	Business Partner Drivers
Internal example: Health-care organization	◆ Technology ◆ Loss of key management personnel	◆ Health-care costs ◆ Change in insurance providers	◆ Rising costs ◆ Decreased cash flow
External example: Health-care organization	◆ Loss of market share ◆ Increase in number of competitors ◆ Lack of available employees (nurses)	◆ Medicare changes ◆ Regulation changes ◆ Cost of medicine	◆ Regulation on product line ◆ Global innovation and development shrinking competitive advantage
Internal:			
External:			

Part B: Facilitation Questions

1. What are the *key* external and internal business drivers in your organization today?

2. How are these drivers likely to change?

3. How consistent have these drivers been? Are these the same drivers you faced three years ago? five years ago? 10 years ago?

4. What type of external changes are you seeing in the world today that may create external and internal business driver impact for your organization?

5. How has your organization responded in the past to changing business drivers?

6. What business drivers do you, your customers, and your business partners share? How might these shared drivers be important to your strategy?

7. What business drivers differ for your customers and business partners? How might these different drivers be important to your strategy?

8. What additional information do you need about the business drivers to react to them more appropriately in your strategy?

9. How are these business drivers reflected in the SWOT analysis?

10. How might these drivers affect the outcomes, goals, and objectives defined in your strategy?

11. How might these drivers affect the future of your organization if not responded to appropriately?

12. How might these drivers affect performance needs across your departments and groups?

13. What is the key external driver affecting your organization? How is that driver influencing your current and future strategy? Does it change the priorities in your outcomes?

14. What is the key internal driver affecting your organization? How is that driver influencing your current and future strategy? Does it change the priorities in your outcomes?

15. What worries or excites you about the business drivers you identified relative to the strategy?

tacted during the work performed in Step 1. Now it's the time to gain their perspective and feedback in looking ahead at the company they are leading, how they define its future, and how the outcomes will assist them in meeting future company needs.

The questions in tool 2.4 can be used as is in your meetings, or you can customize them to fit your organization's culture and needs. First present the information you collected during the business scan; then use these questions as a way to validate your findings with the executives you are interviewing. The second column of tool 2.4 lists the section of the strategic plan to which the question applies. The answer to a question will supply data for that section. You may use just a few of the questions or all of them. It's helpful to organize the responses by strategy section. Grouping all the responses to questions about strategy charter or about tactics will help you analyze them more easily later on. (We'll discuss the analysis of the responses in Step 4.)

If your organization is young or fairly small, you may want to couple these interview questions with the SWOT analysis (worksheet

TOOL 2.4

Suggested Questions for Executive Interviews

Interview Question	Pertinent Strategy Section
What key challenges does our organization face in the future?	Strategy charter
What factors in the business environment itself are forcing change for our organization?	Strategy charter
What global issues will affect our organization's future?	Strategy charter
How will the outcomes of the strategy help our organization in the future?	Strategy charter
What is your major concern about our organization's future and its ability to overcome that concern?	Strategy charter

Interview Question	Pertinent Strategy Section
What major business strategies will require employee support?	Tactical plan
What major business strategies will require technological support?	Tactical plan
What major business strategies will affect our customer base?	Tactical plan
What risks does our organization face in the future?	Description of current environment
What do you think are our key competencies today?	Description of current environment
How do those competencies need to change for the future of our organization?	Tactical plan
What metrics do you think are important to measure the strategy's success in preparing us for the future?	Expected results
What constraints do you see in getting our organization from where it is to where it needs to be in the future?	Tactical plan
What information do you think is the most important to make our case for the strategy?	Findings from research
What do you think our mission statement should reflect?	Mission statement
Do you think our current mission statement paints the right picture?	Mission statement
If you could make one thing happen for our organization's future, what would it be?	Tactical plan
Are there other organizations (in our industry, among our competitors) from which we should gather information; and, if so, what types of information would be beneficial in building our strategy?	Findings from research
What else do you think is important for us to consider regarding the development of the strategy?	Open question

STEP **2**

2.1) to get the executives' views of the organization's strengths, weaknesses, opportunities, and threats from both the organizational and strategic outcome points of view.

Setting Guidelines for Data Collection

As a result of the work done in this step, you and your group should have a better idea of the types of information that will be valuable to review or collect in developing and executing your strategy. More will be discussed on this topic in the next step, but there are a few tasks to wrap up with the strategic planning work group to ensure you are ready to initiate the data collection step (Step 3). First, use worksheet 2.3 as a checklist of information that would be valuable in the strategic planning process but that has not been collected. Next, list the information that is available, who has it or will be responsible for collecting it, and when that information is due to the strategic development group leader. It may be helpful to use worksheet 2.4 to track the data collection efforts and responsibilities.

It may be helpful now to establish guidelines and processes you'll use in gathering information for the strategic plan. Keep these guidelines in mind and follow them wherever appropriate to ensure that this significant body of company data is handled safely and securely. Here are the guidelines we think you'll find most useful:

1. Keep the original data (unaltered) on a disk in a safe, secure, and environmentally sound location.
2. Hold a master copy of the data in password-protected files. Remember that this is strategic information for your organization and therefore highly valuable. It's important to know that the integrity of the data is preserved for potential future use.
3. Keep a back-up copy in an approved off-site location.
4. Make copies of the master file for data manipulation. To safeguard against accidental or intentional corruption, don't use the master copy as a working document.
5. At this point in the planning process, create a data-tracking notebook in which you record what data are be-

WORKSHEET 2.3

Checklist of Information Needed for Strategic Planning

Information	Should the Information Be Collected?	
Current environment data	Yes ☐	No ☐
Best practices information	Yes ☐	No ☐
Competitor information	Yes ☐	No ☐
Industry benchmarking information	Yes ☐	No ☐
Financial information	Yes ☐	No ☐
Future trend information	Yes ☐	No ☐
Customer information	Yes ☐	No ☐
Organization's strategy, vision, and goals information	Yes ☐	No ☐
Business partner information	Yes ☐	No ☐

ing collected and where they are located. (Keeping copies of worksheet 2.4 in this notebook may be helpful.) As procedures for data collection and analysis are created, add them to the notebook. If any data collection changes are needed, note them as well.

◆ ◆ ◆

In the following steps you will gather and analyze additional information that will help you develop tactics to achieve meaningful results for your customers, partners, and stakeholders.

WORKSHEET 2.4

Data Collection and Accountability Tracking Sheet

Instructions: Use this sheet to list the information you want to gather for your strategy plan development, and note the person accountable for collecting and delivering it to the work group. A sample entry is included to illustrate its use.

Data	Data Type/Format	Source	Data Origination Date	Data Location	Person Accountable for Collecting Data
Example: Organizational history	*Video (orientation for new employees)*	*HR department*	*2/17/07*	*Resource room*	*C. Tucker, HR director*

Collecting Relevant Data

OVERVIEW

Planning your data collection

Choosing among types of data collection

Identifying data sources

Maximizing data validity and reliability

As a result of the work you completed in Steps 1 and 2, you are ready to begin collecting the data needed for strategic planning decision making. Data collection is often the most time-intensive part of strategic planning. If it's not done wisely, valuable time will be wasted on unnecessary activities or error-ridden data will be used to make important decisions that will affect the organization's short- and long-term health. Although you want the data you collect to be as complete as possible, don't collect it simply because you feel you must or because it seems like a good idea. The effectiveness of the final strategic plan depends on the quality—more than the quantity—of the data used in building strategy tactics.

Data always are needed as soon as possible. Typically, you're under pressure to complete the strategy so you can execute the plan. Most likely, you have limited resources and want to spend your time implementing changes rather than gathering data. In our discussion of this third step in the planning process, we'll focus on the tools used to collect relevant data for developing and supporting the strategic plan. Specifically, we'll address the following topics:

- planning for data collection
- choosing among types of data collection
- identifying sources of preexisting information
- maximizing the validity and reliability of the data.

The goals of data collection are to help the organization make critical decisions regarding its strategy and to identify the tactics it should deploy to best meet its long- and short-term goals and objectives. The data collected should help prioritize work and resources and help build the case that executing the identified tactics is important to the organization's health.

In collecting data for strategic planning, most time is spent in identifying needed information, soliciting original data, and designing and testing collection instruments. In this step we'll provide resources to reduce the time you spend on these activities, thereby enabling you to complete Step 3 as quickly as possible.

Case Examples: Collecting Data

Each organization has different needs, and each strategic plan requires the gathering of different information. The following case examples demonstrate how unique sets of circumstances drove different approaches to collecting the data needed to develop a strategic plan.

Learning from Surveys and Interviews

Maintaining a competitive advantage is a key driver for American Vista Software, which supplies software for the computer design industry. It's a highly competitive field. In the past two years, the company has acquired 10 other firms and merged cultures and product lines. There are plans for more acquisitions.

During the business scan completed in Step 2, it became clear that the organization's infrastructure and process documentation were not well communicated. Although employees often discussed among themselves the lack of documentation and processes, they

POINTER

Data collection is often the most time-intensive part of strategic planning. If it's not done wisely, you'll waste valuable time or use error-ridden data to make crucial decisions.

never had the opportunity to articulate the problem in a way that made senior management aware of the company cost of not having sound documentation and processes. Now, using surveys and interviews, American Vista is working to determine what tactics to use to document the processes easily, keep the documentation current, and ensure that employees know how to access and use the documentation. Although using an electronic performance management system has been discussed to answer the short-term need, senior management wants a long-term strategy for process development and documentation that encompasses all facets of the organization, from operations to sales to administration.

Getting a Picture of What's Available and What's Needed in the Field

Capital Hills Insurance has been in business more than 60 years. During the past year, the company reorganized and completed several complex initiatives, including updating its overall technology plan. All of the field offices have new computer equipment, and all sales associates now have a personal computer. This was part of an outcome identified in the former strategic plan.

With this new technology, the strategic planning group decided that the sales materials and process would be more leading-edge if field personnel had sales literature and product information available on automated systems at their workstations. Before this is finalized as an objective for modernizing the salesforce, however, the strategic planning group needs to complete these data-collection activities:

◆ a literature search to identify the best practices in the industry and the practices used by key competitors

♦ interviews with the sales management, marketing, regulation, and materials development departments to identify the best processes, and other information to incorporate in the process itself

♦ focus groups with the salesforce to identify what will work best for them and their clients, and how the process should work in the field—including the initial and ongoing training efforts.

Planning for Data Collection

Making plans for data collection typically includes these nine activities:

1. Defining the criteria and outcomes of the data collection.
2. Identifying who will use the information and how it will be used.
3. Determining what information is needed.
4. Deciding if there will be multiple uses for the data and, if so, what they are.
5. Determining when the data will be needed.
6. Determining the resources available to gather the information.
7. Identifying the approaches to be used to gather the information.
8. Identifying methods to ensure the data are reliable and accurate.
9. Deciding who will collect the data and what they will need to support them (training, technology, administrative support, and so forth).

The data collected should be appropriate for use in developing a strategic plan and should be valid and credible. Before you devise a plan to collect your data, be sure you've identified all of the data needed to build the strategic plan. In Step 2 of the planning process, your group created a list of the types of information it believed to be significant. At this point, finalize that list and select the most effective and expeditious ways to obtain the information.

Review what you learned from the business scan, including the SWOT analysis and the business drivers, and then answer the following questions:

- What information do you need to build a plan that is future oriented, links to your organization's business, and supports your customers' needs?
- How will you know if you have the correct information?
- Do you need to validate the information? If so, with whom and how?
- What information will help you make a case for the outcomes, goals, and objectives you have identified?
- What information can you collect that would be contrary to the outcomes, goals, and objectives you have identified?
- What information will help you make informed decisions specific to the strategic plan and its ultimate mission and tactics?
- What information about your customers is important to consider in building a strategic plan? Are your customers' demographics and product needs consistent with your plans?
- What information about your business partners is important to consider? Are there time or economic constraints relative to your partners that you need to take into account?
- What data did your stakeholders and sponsors provide that give you insight into the organization's direction to ensure that the tactical plans you build are visionary and appropriate to the business needs?
- What business initiatives discussed by the sponsors and stakeholders can the organization develop products, programs, and services to support?
- Is there missing information regarding your customers, stakeholders, business partners, or sponsors that is critical to building the strategic plan?
- Does one set of information (customer data, for example) support or contradict another set (business partners data, for example), and how is this important to the strategic plan?

When you believe you've identified all of the data that needs to be collected, develop a plan that documents how the data collection process will proceed. Ultimately, to collect data you should know

◆ what data will be collected

◆ the type of data that will be collected (past/present/future trends)

◆ who will be accountable for collecting the data

◆ how the data will be collected (the methodology)

◆ what will be done with the data when they are collected (how they will be used)

◆ why the data are important (or the rationale for collecting the data)

◆ any potential problems that may affect the validity of the data (small sampling population, potentially biased collector, easily misrepresented data, and the like).

Worksheet 3.1 will help you keep the answers to these questions in mind as you formulate a plan for collecting your data. When collection is finished, place the worksheet in the strategic plan binder for future reference if needed.

As noted in the example in worksheet 3.1, subjective data may be collected through focus groups. Before you create your collection plan, decide if you should institute controls to ensure the integrity of the data—controls such as comparing multiple samples or benchmarking like organizations to compare the focus group data.

It's also important at this point to ensure that the data you are collecting will meet the outcomes, goals, and objectives of the strategic plan. You may find it helpful here to review worksheet 2.1, which you completed in the previous step. Update it with any new information that links to your outcomes, goals, and objectives. If data you've recently identified doesn't align with the outcomes, then decide if it can be skipped or if you have overlooked an outcome needed for the strategic plan. This may require some reworking of what you completed in Steps 1 and 2 and an accompanying validation with your group and senior management, but more often than not, you'll find that everything aligns.

WORKSHEET 3.1

Building a Data Collection Plan

Instructions: Use this worksheet to keep track of all the data you will collect before you develop your strategic plan. Understanding the data you seek will help you devise an effective and speedy collection strategy. An example is provided for illustration purposes.

Data to Be Collected	Rationale for Collection	Final Use for Collected Data	Type of Data (Past, Present, Future Trends)	Colection Methodology	Individual(s) Accountable	Potential Sources of Error or Bias
Example: Sales-force opinions	*To gain input for sales process and training*	*To build new process for using field technology*	*Present and future trends*	*Focus groups*	*K. Crew and L. Miu*	*Subjective collection methods*

STEP
3

With the data identified and aligned to the outcomes, you are ready to create your system for managing data collection. In tool 3.1 you'll find questions to answer for each piece of information you will collect. Looking at this type of detail for every bit of data you collect often reveals issues or problems. If identified early, these issues and problems usually can be resolved or supplemented with other data. By planning ahead and addressing possible problems at the outset, you reduce the time you spend on data collection because you have to contact the data sources only once to ob-

TOOL 3.1

Questions for Defining the Scope of the Data to Be Collected

Factor	Questions to Define the Scope
Type of data	What is to be collected? *Sample answers:* market information, productivity statistics
Age of data	Are the data from the past or the present, or are they future trend projections?
Data measurement units	What is the method of measurement for the data? *Sample answers:* percentage, count, totals
Purpose of data collection	Why are these specific data needed? What is the rationale for gathering them?
Data insight	When the data are presented, what do we expect them to tell us?
Type of measure	Is the measure an input, a process, or an output?
Strategic outcome	To what outcome are these data linked?
Use of data	How will the data be used, and what will be done with them?
Individual(s) accountable for data	Who is ultimately responsible for collecting these data?

Factor	Questions to Define the Scope
Location for data collection	Where will the data be collected? *Sample answers:* on site, via the Internet, at a scheduled meeting
Method of data collection	What method will be used to collect the data? *Sample answers:* a system count, an existing or developed productivity report, a survey, a focus group, an industry study. How will the collection be completed? Who will develop the survey? What criteria will be used in gathering focus group participants?
Data collection schedule	What is the timeframe for the data collection? When will it begin and within what period of time will it be completed?
Data recording method	How will the data be recorded? *Sample answers:* on preformatted observation sheets, on an Internet survey form
Quality control	How will the data be kept confidential? How will errors and bias be identified and reported?

STEP **3**

tain everything you need, not repeatedly to collect data that were missed the first time through.

It's helpful to document the data collection in a summary record. You may have to create a more fully developed plan if your organization requires it, or if great amounts of data will be collected, but even a simple summary document is a good checklist. It's a high-level plan and should be kept in your strategic planning notebook. Example 3.1 illustrates a data collection summary record.

Choosing Data Collection Methods

There are several different methods you can use to gather data, and more than one of them can be used to select the same data. Understanding the various methods and their respective advantages and

EXAMPLE 3.1

High-Level Data Collection Summary Record

Data	Source	Collection Method	Unit of Measurement	Collection Steps	Person Accountable	Schedule
Best-practice information on hiring	Industry data from First Research	Industry profile information	Trend summary	1. Request profile information 2. Review data 3. Summarize data by competition 4. Enter data and compile	J. Gennet D. Michels	1/6–10/08
Current sales manager interview process	Interviews scheduled for new sales managers	Observations	Observation summaries Counts of data	1. Create data observation sheet 2. Get interview schedule 3. Conduct observations 4. Convert observation into data sheets 5. Enter data and compile	D. Michels K. Roget R. Hernandez B. Kiele	1/15–2/20/08
Current sales manager input	Sales managers with one to three years in position	Interviews	Counts, totals, and summaries of input	1. Determine sample 2. Send email 3. Develop interview protocol 4. Train interviewers 5. Schedule interviews 6. Conduct interviews 7. Convert notes to data entry forms 8. Enter data	R. Schmidt D. Smith K. Geilsler	1/15–2/20/08

disadvantages will help you make better decisions about how best to collect the data you need. You will want to consider such things as

- availability of resources
- quality and quantity of available information
- cost of development and data collection methods
- availability and consistency of technology and other data-gathering methods across locations
- location of the data (Internet, people, library, a service or consulting agency, and so forth)
- characteristics of your sample (For example, if people form your sample, what is their ability to access and complete surveys or be involved in focus groups?)
- data source (some resources are better for certain topics than others)
- collection schedule (that is, how time sensitive your data collection is)
- required response rate (For example, if you're using a survey or a focus group, how many responses do you need per question to establish data validity?)
- burden on respondent (that is, the degree to which the response depends on his or her effort)
- complexity (that is, how deep or detailed the data must be)
- possibility of bias introduced by the person doing the data collection
- control of the data (that is, how sure you are that the data are from the desired source).

The most common methods of data collection used in strategic planning are listed in table 3.1, and evaluated relative to the considerations listed above. Using this table to compare the advantages and disadvantages of the methods against your data requirements will help you quickly decide which method(s) to use.

There are other methods that are more technology driven and generally more automated. Because these methods usually are unbiased, the data mined from them are extremely valuable. One word of caution—if these methods are not currently available in your organization, the cost of implementing them solely for the purpose of

TABLE 3.1

Considerations for Selecting Common Data Collection Methods

Considerations	Background Research	Mail Survey	Telephone Survey	Web Survey	Face-to-face Survey	Focus Group	Observation
Resource skill level	Medium	Medium	Medium	High	High	High	High
Cost	Usually low	Low	Moderate	Depends on resources, but can be low	High	Moderate	High
Availability of use	Readily available	Readily available	Readily available	Moderately available	Moderately to readily available	Moderately available	Not readily available
Data location	Widely available	Widely available	Widely available	Widely available	Limited availability	Limited availability	Limited availability
Time sensitivity	Low	High	High	Medium	High	High	High
Response rate	Not applicable	Low	Medium	Medium	High	High	High
Respondent burden	No burden	High burden	Moderate burden	Moderate burden	Low burden	Low burden	Low burden

Depth and level of data	High	Low	Low	Low	Medium	High	High
Bias possibility	Moderate risk	Low risk	Moderate risk	Low risk	Moderate risk	High risk	Moderate risk
Data control	Source is certain	Source uncertain	Source is certain	Source is only somewhat certain	Source is certain	Source is certain	Source is certain

gathering information for strategic planning may be prohibitive. Table 3.2 lists some of these methods and explains how they can be used in data collection efforts.

When you've identified the needed data and the optimum methods for gathering them, you're ready to develop your collection tools. Let's get a more detailed look at focus groups, interviews, surveys, and background research.

Focus Groups and Interviews

Specific groups of people—business partners, current or prospective customers, or competitors—have information that you need and

TABLE 3.2

Technology-Driven Data Collection Methods

Method	Data Collection Use
Weblogs, or blogs	Blogs can be used to research an idea or ask a question and gain feedback. For example, if you set up a blog for your field sales people to report how they are using their computers, they can give you that information and/or make suggestions about what other computer programs and materials might assist them in selling.
Kiosks, touch-sensitive screens	By placing kiosks in malls, recreation areas, grocery stores, or other appropriate venues, you can conduct spontaneous surveys, or you can provide specific information to a person who then can react on the spot. For example, asking a question such as, Would you buy a printer today if it was on sale for $250? will elicit potential customer responses to product pricing. Product features, pricing, and many other types of information can be gathered with touch-sensitive response screens.
Optical mark recognition	Written characters can be scanned into electronic data collection vehicles so that information from hand-written customer surveys can be collated digitally.

Table 3.2, continued

Method	Data Collection Use
Intelligent character recognition (ICR)	After data collectors use paper-based forms with their interviewees, the ICR scans the forms and enters the data into an electronic database that can be downloaded as needed.
Bar codes	Whereas bar codes on products in stores help manage inventory, they also can be used to determine what types of customers purchase certain products and at what prices. The capture of product and pricing data for each customer enables a company to know where and when products are being purchased and by whom.
Data capture	Cookies (small data files created by a Web server and stored on your computer to allow a Website to recognize you and keep track of your preferences) and electronic tracking systems operate in the background to capture data from personal and organizational computers. Within an organization, data capture lets you see, for example, how specific data are accessed or how often product information is used in a sale. This technology also can be used to gather data from prospective customers as they complete Web-based forms before gaining access to your Website. And it can be used for online surveys.

that you can't get elsewhere. Focus groups or interviews work best with specific individuals who have valuable information (for example, the business managers from five organizations in your industry) or with a small and narrowly defined group (for example, 5–15 randomly chosen customers who fit a specific demographic profile).

Whether you conduct interviews or focus groups depends on several factors. Table 3.3 discusses the differences between the two methods.

The mechanics for both methods are very similar. The first task is to list your objectives for the focus group or interview. Then select the sample of respondents by determining the participant characteristics you will need to meet your objectives. You may want to target

TABLE 3.3

Comparison of Focus Groups and Interviews

Focus Group Characteristics	Interview Characteristics
Use planned discussion in a group to gain perceptions on a defined area of content.	Use planned discussion one-on-one to gain perceptions on a defined area of content.
Environment is nonthreatening.	Environment is nonthreatening.
Participants share ideas and perceptions and influence each other by piggybacking on ideas.	Participants share ideas and perceptions in a private conversation.
The group hears and responds to ideas.	The interviewer is a passive participant, and conversation is very confidential.
The interviewer is not usually in a directive role.	The interviewer is usually in a directive role.
More people can be interviewed in a shorter timeframe.	Method is time consuming if more than three or four people are to be interviewed.

specific interviewees (for example, senior managers, prospects for new products, current customers), or you can use sampling techniques (such as random or stratified sampling) to select participants. You'll find sampling tools for this purpose on the Internet, and here are some good sources to consult:

- ◆ Creative Research Systems, www.surveysystem.com
- ◆ Survey Guy, www.surveyguy.com
- ◆ Custominsight, www.custominsight.com/articles/random-sample-calulator.

The third and perhaps most challenging step to conducting a focus group or interview is to develop the guide (or script). Your focus groups and interviews should be as consistent as possible so the data you gather from them is more easily analyzed. To ensure that the questions or order are not confusing or leading, you should develop a guide to keep the discussion on track. The guide will contain an opening statement (usually the objective of the research), the questions (with follow-up probes), and the closing remarks.

In developing an interview or focus group guide, you first need to answer the following questions:

◆ What do you want to know as a result of the interview or focus group?

◆ How will you sequence the questions for the interview or focus group?

◆ How much detail do you wish to solicit from the interviewee or participants?

◆ How long do you think the interview or focus group should last?

◆ How should you word the questions?

Review examples of interview or focus group scripts with objectives that are similar to yours. Two sites on the Internet offer examples of interview and focus group scripts and additional resources: Flashlight Evaluation Handbook (www.learningobjects .wesleyan.edu/downloads/focus_groups_protocol.htm) and Office of Research Ethics (www.research.uwaterloo.ca/ethics/human /application/101samples.htm). Identify what was successful about those scripts and, if problems existed, try to determine why. Then duplicate the successes.

Although interviews and focus groups usually use qualitative questions, you can gather some quantitative data using questions with prespecified multiple-choice or ranking responses (such as high/medium/low or always/sometimes/never). Here's an example of a question with prespecified multiple-choice responses:

If you were given a choice of spending a $500 bonus on one of the four items listed, what would you spend it on: (1) technology, (2) travel, (3) education, or (4) entertainment?

Here's an example of an open-ended question seeking essentially the same information but with no limiting factors included:

STEP 3

If you were given a $500 bonus and had a choice about how to spend it, what would you buy?

Tool 3.2 defines and exemplifies six question types that are most commonly used in interviews and focus groups.

Typically you will design the interview or focus group questions to begin with less-sensitive or more easily answered questions, such as demographics or background. (Remember that demographic questions can quickly become tedious, especially in a focus group, so

TOOL 3.2

Six Commonly Used Types of Focus Group or Interview Questions

Type of Question	Definition	Examples
Background or demographics	Asks identifying characteristics of those interviewed (typically education, role, business unit)	• What is your role at XYZ Corporation? • Do you have children at home who are under 18?
Experience	Seeks details of a situation or experience	• Tell me about the sales training you have had in the past. • How often do you use [*product*]?
Sensory	Questions what has been seen, heard, felt, or touched	• When you walk into one of our stores, what is the first thing you see?
Knowledge	Assesses what information or knowledge is present	• Describe for me what I would hear the customer service representative say to a customer calling about a product issue. • What circumstances enable a customer to be eligible for fee waivers? • What are the procedures for dealing with a safety hazard in our organization?

Tool 3.2, continued

Type of Question	Definition	Examples
Feeling	Determines how the interviewee feels about a topic	• What is your confidence level when making a customer call on investment portfolios? • To what extent do you feel concerned when providing a credit card number to a company online?
Opinion or value	Determines what the interviewee thinks about an issue	• Did the automated phone system make the customer service experience more satisfactory? • What product changes would you recommend?

try to limit them.) It's usually easier to ask experience questions first and address opinion questions later after you have established a level of trust.

One of the most important things to remember when writing questions for interviews or focus groups is that *each question should focus on a single idea.* The question, What are our key business drivers, and how do you think we can overcome the issues they create? contains too many elements and will hinder meaningful discussion. Asking the two parts of this question as separate questions will be more effective. The number of *why* questions you include in the guide should be limited because they tend to irritate interviewees or participants when they are asked repeatedly.

When you've developed the questions, three activities remain:

1. Pilot test the process with a few members of the target population using a prototype or preliminary version of the guide. Identify any problems, such as misunderstood questions, and revise the script to fix them.

2. Conduct the interviews or focus groups, and track the responses using a previously agreed method to ensure con-

sistency and make analysis easier later on. Whereas one person is needed to conduct interviews, two people from your team will be required for a focus group—one to facilitate and one to act as scribe.

3. Compile the notes for data analysis.

Example 3.2 is a guide used in interviews with stakeholders. The guide defines the purpose of each question and provides suggested probes for digging deeper during the interview.

Surveys

Surveys offer confidentiality to respondents and can be administered to large groups, typically a customer group or an employee base. They also are a good method for collecting data from respondents in a variety of locations. After you've identified the need for and objectives of a survey, your next actions are

- setting a budget and a schedule
- identifying the sample size and any participation criteria (for example, demographics)
- deciding if you need help in designing the survey (for example, technical expertise, subject-matter expertise)
- designing the survey
- testing the survey
- implementing the survey
- coding the completed surveys or entering the results into a database.

Here are few tips for successful surveying:

- Keep the survey as short as possible. If you can make it one page, do so; two pages is the maximum desirable size.
- Provide a small reward either for everyone who returns the survey or for a limited number of respondents. (If possible, make that number the amount of responses you need for the survey sample size to be valid.)
- Try to make distribution and collection as time efficient as possible. Email is extremely efficient, especially for internal surveys.

EXAMPLE 3.2

Interview Guide

Introductory Remarks: [*Start by introducing yourself.*] This interview is being conducted with you and others in the organization. As you know, we are in the process of developing and executing [or revising] a strategic plan. To ensure that the final plan is closely linked with our business and that the products and services we offer will continue to support our customers and employees, we have developed a 10-question interview. As I told you when I made this appointment, I expect this interview to take no longer than 45 minutes. Do you have any questions for me before we begin?

Question	Purpose	Suggested Probes
1. What do you see as our organization's mission?	To help understand how the mission is seen or how it needs to be revised	• What is the core reason our organization exists? • Is that reflected in the mission? • Could you put that in one to three sentences?
2. How do you feel this mission aligns with the way our organization works?	To uncover any disconnects between the mission and the "real" organization; to help link the mission to the organization	• What is missing in our mission statement? • Do you think we "walk the talk" relative to the mission statement? • How should the mission statement change?
3. What key challenges face our organization in the future?	To ensure that the outcomes have tactics that will meet these challenges	• What barriers exist to our organization's success (externally, internally)? • What about this challenge is unique to our organization?
4. What factors in the business environment are forcing change in our organization?	To identify and validate business drivers	• What business drivers are forcing the business to change (for example, increased competition, lack of resources, decreased revenue)? • How do these factors/drivers affect our organization? • What or who is responsible for these drivers?

continued on next page

STEP
3

Example 3.2, continued

Question	Purpose	Suggested Probes
5. What do you think is the biggest risk to our organization in the future?	To uncover organizational vulnerabilities	• What internal or external influences pose a threat to the organization? Why? • How do these risks affect our organization?
6. In what ways do you think our products and services could provide more value to our customers?	To understand how others feel the organization can improve its customer link	• What is the value of our products and services to the customer? • How could this be increased?
7. What are our organization's core strengths?	To determine what others think the organization does best	• What do you think we do best as an organization? • How do you know that? • What do you think is important about these strengths?
8. What do you think is the biggest human resource challenge we face today?	To determine what others think needs to happen for employees	• What is challenging about this? • In what ways can we meet this challenge?
9. What do you think is the biggest technological challenge we face today?	To determine what others think needs to happen with regard to technology	• What is challenging about this? • In what ways can we meet this challenge?
10. What do you think is the biggest competitive challenge we face today?	To gain a perspective on what the organization needs to do to be more competitive	• What is challenging about this? • In what ways can we meet this challenge?

You should schedule one or two person-days to create and test your survey. Survey writing takes time. First you must identify what you want to ask and then you write and rewrite the questions to ensure they are clear, concise, and not misleading. Tool 3.3 provides guidelines for developing survey questions, along with examples of survey items that are poorly written and items that are better.

Before testing your survey, you may want to compare it against the standard criteria for effective questions listed in worksheet 3.2.

A sample survey is presented in example 3.3. This survey was used to identify management styles existing in the sales department.

The Internet is another tool that is helpful in both survey development and survey delivery. There are several services that will help you deliver surveys across the Web (and some actually will do the design). This is especially helpful if you're trying to do a blind survey with customers or prospects, and don't want any preconceived ideas to form because the respondents relate the survey to your organization. Here are some of these services:

◆ ZapSurvey, www.zapsurvey.com
◆ Zoomerang, www.zoomerang.com
◆ Vanguard Software Corporation, Vista Online Surveys, www.vista-survey.com
◆ Nooro Online Research, www.nooro.com.

Background Research

Background research is best used to gather information on trends, the marketplace, competitors, or other critical topics. Much of this information is readily available. The conclusions and recommendations for your strategy's tactics most likely will be based on the information and themes revealed by this research.

The biggest problem with background research is spending too much time obtaining unnecessary data. Setting objectives and being realistic about what you want to know and the sources you are exploring can help you avoid this problem. Effective background research begins with these three activities:

TOOL 3.3

Guidelines for Developing Survey Questions

Guideline	Poorly Written Items	Improved Items
Use wording that is simple and to the point.	Do you remember when you last took a class from the training and development department? Was it less than six months ago?	Have you taken a class from training and development in the last six months?
Use wording that is neutral and does not bias the respondent.	Some think that only classroom delivery is effective for training and nothing else works. What do you think?	Which of the following alternative delivery programs would you rather participate in? [Delivery programs are listed.]
Be careful not to influence respondents when providing explanations.	What are your top three priorities for employee development this year (for example, leadership training, technical training, sales training)?	Training and development is working on its program delivery plan for the next year. To ensure that we meet your needs, list your top three priorities for employee development this year.
Provide response intervals that will give you meaningful information.	How many employees report to you? ___ 1 ___ 5 ___ 10 ___ 15	How many employees report to you? ___ Less than 5 ___ 6–10 ___ 11–15 ___ More than 15

Principle	Example	Example
When using prespecified responses to a question, provide no more than 10 responses to avoid confusion.	Which of the following classes have you taken in the past six months? [All 20 classes are listed.]	Which of the following management classes have you taken in the past six months? [Six management classes are listed, with *None of the above* included.]
The alternative responses should be logically ordered if using intervals, or randomly ordered if using a list of responses.	How would you rate your experience with paper-based self-study for interview training in the past? ___ OK ___ Poor ___ Great	Select the delivery methods you would prefer for interview training: ___ Web seminar ___ Classroom ___ Paper-based self-study
When using a Likert scale, define five, seven, or nine points to avoid confusion.	Please rate the opportunities you have to gain increased responsibility in your job, on a scale of 1 to 7, where 1 is *No opportunities* and 7 is *Often given opportunities.*	Please rate the opportunities you have to gain increased responsibility in your job: 1—Never offered 2—Rarely offered 3—Seldom offered 4—Sometimes offered 5—Regularly offered

STEP

3

WORKSHEET 3.2

Criteria for Judging the Effectiveness of Your Survey Questions

Criterion	Does Question Meet Criterion?
The respondents understand the questions (the pilot-testing should reveal this).	Yes ☐ No ☐
If response choices are used, they are clear, and they elicit the desired information.	Yes ☐ No ☐
The questions and responses are comprehensive, and they cover a reasonably complete range of answers.	Yes ☐ No ☐
The questions motivate responses for all of the information that you have identified as important. There is no redundancy, and nothing is missing.	Yes ☐ No ☐
The survey is an acceptable length.	Yes ☐ No ☐
The questions honor the participants' privacy.	Yes ☐ No ☐
The survey avoids asking participants for information that is gathered another way. For example, if the employee number indicates his or her division, the survey should not ask for the employee's division location.	Yes ☐ No ☐
The level of wording is acceptable for the audience (for example, highly technical language is not used for novices; language level does not exceed grade 8 for a general population).	Yes ☐ No ☐

1. Creating questions that define the research. For example, what are the parameters of the search? (Go back to your outcomes, goals, and objectives for assistance with this.) In the second case example we offered at the beginning of this step, the parameters were best practices in alternatives to classroom delivery.

EXAMPLE 3.3

A Survey of Management Styles

	No Opinion	Strongly Disagree	Disagree	Somewhat Disagree	Somewhat Agree	Agree	Strongly Agree
1. Sales managers in this organization often							
lead by example	☐	☐	☐	☐	☐	☐	☐
provide feedback on sales process often	☐	☐	☐	☐	☐	☐	☐
encourage new ideas to increase sales	☐	☐	☐	☐	☐	☐	☐
know the products and services	☐	☐	☐	☐	☐	☐	☐
keep others up-to-date on new products and services	☐	☐	☐	☐	☐	☐	☐
2. The depth of information on products and prospects I receive from my manager has met my needs in the past.	☐	☐	☐	☐	☐	☐	☐
3. I receive performance feedback from my manager at least once a month.	☐	☐	☐	☐	☐	☐	☐
4. My manager is available through a variety of methods (cell phone, email, voice messaging).	☐	☐	☐	☐	☐	☐	☐
5. My manager responds to my questions and calls within 24 hours during the workweek.	☐	☐	☐	☐	☐	☐	☐

EXAMPLE 3.4

Research Plan Based on Research Objectives

Research Objective	Information Source	Collection Method	Timeframe
To understand customers' preferences for delivery of training	Random selection of the A-list customers	Survey	12 work-days
To gain a better understanding of customers' technical capabilities	Random selection of the A-list customers	Survey	12 work-days
To identify what methods competitors are using for product training	◆ Internet ◆ Marketing and sales organization studies ◆ Periodicals	Research study	4 work-days
To identify what best-practice methods other industries are using for product training	◆ Internet ◆ Marketing and sales organization studies ◆ Periodicals	Research study	4 work-days

2. Identifying the resources or sources you will use. Associations or industry groups, publications, other companies, the Internet, and technical libraries are good possibilities.
3. Identifying your research method. Examples include a literature search and benchmarking an organization.

Examples 3.4 and 3.5 illustrate, respectively, a research plan based on research objectives and a plan based on research questions. Document the questions or objectives for each of your data gathering, the sources you'll use, the data collection method, and a timeframe for completing the data gathering.

Tool 3.4 can help you target the background information you need for your plan and the best sources for gathering it.

Here are some helpful tips for your data search:
◆ Identify all the key words that define or relate to the topic you're researching—for example, quality, total quality man-

agement, Deming, team management. Use these terms in Web search engines and book indexes to locate information on your topic.

◆ Identify all the companies that are successful at this type of program, are considered your competition, or have best practices you would like to learn more about.

EXAMPLE 3.5

Research Plan Based on Research Questions

Research Definition Question	Planned Source	Research Method
1. What in South America makes the most sense for our expansion?	◆ Multilateral Investment Fund ◆ National Political Infrastructure and Foreign Direct Investment ◆ World Advertising Research Center (www.warc.com)	Literature search
2. What approaches to human resource benefits is our competition planning for the future?	◆ First Research ◆ InfoScouts (www.infoscouts.com) ◆ Dun & Bradstreet	Mixed approaches
3. What expected barriers or obstacles are there in introducing new technology to our customer?	◆ Customer demographics ◆ Benchmarking Exchange (www.benchnet.com)	Benchmarking
4. What are the trends in marketing to new prospects?	◆ Marketing organizations/associations ◆ NetSuite (www.netsuite.com)	Internal marketing study
5. What are the most common quality issues in introducing new technology?	◆ Quality organizations/associations ◆ Tunu Pure Web Searching (www.tunu.com)	Mixed approaches
6. What are today's best practices in the industry?	◆ The Hackett Group (www.thehackettgroup.com) ◆ Benchmarking & Best Practices Council	Benchmarking

◆ Complete an industry search in your own industry or an industry known to be successful in this type of program, or both.

TOOL 3.4

Sources for Targeting the Background Information You Need

Information Needed	Rationale	Data Sources
Trend information	To plan for the future or to target goals for professional practices	• Internet • Best practices organizations • Professional associations
Competition practices	To determine what your competition is doing that perhaps you should (or should not) be doing	• Internet • Periodicals • Professional associations
Customer information	To identify what your customers want or need and how they prefer to receive information or training	• Customer or customer group
Business partner information	To identify what business partners are doing, what their plans are, and how you can support them	• Business partner
Specific requirements for a program or technology	To identify what is needed to support a certification program, to do testing, to implement e-learning, to do a results evaluation, and so forth	• Internet • Periodicals • Professional associations • Best practices organizations • Expert in area of requirements
Benchmarking or best practices information	To identify what is considered a best practice or to gather baseline information for comparison with a group doing the same thing	• Internet • Periodicals • Professional associations • Best practices organizations • Benchmarking groups

- Complete a search by type of periodical or service—for example, a search of *Harvard Business Review* for like topics.
- Conduct a search using your business drivers as search terms.

Identifying Preexisting Information

Frequently you can save time in Step 3 by identifying the data that already exist and the source of that data. If you're trying to pin down specific information within your organization, try the following resources:

- internal communications (for example, newsletters, event management, internal communications)
- marketing
- HR recruitment
- directory or information services
- quality improvement department.

Types of data typically found within an organization or externally from research resources are listed in table 3.4. The first column lists the types of information you may be seeking, and the second column lists common sources of that type of data. You can use this table to jump-start the gathering of preexisting information and to save you time and other resources. Although not exhaustive, this list may help you identify where specific information is located.

Maximizing Validity and Reliability

Whether you're doing an interview, running a focus group, sending out a survey, or doing background research, conducting a trial is the best way to ensure that your data are valid (or sound) and reliable (or dependable). By conducting a trial you will ensure that the audience you have chosen is not biased and has the characteristics you need to get the data you require. A trial also ensures that the instrument or method you're using will provide the data you want. In this way you can find out beforehand if the key search term you used located data you didn't need or if a survey question gathers unusable data.

TABLE 3.4

Potential Sources of Preexisting Data

Type of Information	Potential Sources
Industry norms, trends, competitive information	◆ Industry associations (generally can be located via the Internet)
Training norms, trends, research information	◆ International Society for Performance Improvement (www.ispi.org) ◆ American Society for Training & Development (www.astd.org) ◆ Training SuperSite (www.trainingsupersite.com) ◆ Brandon Hall (www.brandon-hall.com) ◆ The Masie Center (www.masie.com)
HR norms, trends, and research information	◆ Hr-esource.com (www.hr-esource.com) ◆ Hrfree.com (www.hrfree.com) ◆ Human Resource Development (www.humanresourcedevelopment.start4all.com) ◆ Society for Human Resource Management (www.shrm.org)
Best practices, benchmarking, and the like	◆ American Productivity and Quality Center (www.apqc.org) ◆ American Society for Training & Development Benchmarking Forum (www.astd.org) ◆ Benchmarking Exchange (www.benchnet.com) ◆ Benchmarking & Best Practices Council ◆ Electronic Frontier Foundation (www.eff.org) ◆ Gantthead (www.gantthead.com) ◆ International Stormwater Best Management Practices Database (www.bmpdatabase.org) ◆ The Data Administration Newsletter (www.tdan.com) ◆ www.pearsonncs.com ◆ LexisNexis (www.lexisnexis.com) ◆ Business.com (www.business.com)
General research	◆ ERIC Clearinghouse (www.ericacve.org) ◆ Conference Board Research Publications (www.conference-board.org)

Table 3.4, continued

Type of Information	Potential Sources
	◆ International Data Corporation (www.idc.org) ◆ Google search engine (www.google.com) ◆ Ask search engine (www.ask.com)
Customer data	◆ Sales or marketing departments
Organizational financial results and history	◆ Shareholder communications or investor relations department (sometimes part of the finance or accounting department; may also be in marketing)
Processes and procedures	◆ Internal communications, technical writing department
Industry data and global information	◆ Global Insight (www.globalinsight.com) ◆ Elliott Wave International (www.elliottwave.com) ◆ Industry Insight (www.industryinsight.co.za)
Financial forecasting	◆ Kiplinger (www.kiplinger.com) ◆ Business.com (www.business.com) ◆ Elsevier Publishing (www.elsevier.com) ◆ Commerce-Database Business Directory (www.commerce-database.com) ◆ Lonee Corporation (www.lonee.com) ◆ Hoover's, Inc. (www.hoovers.com) ◆ Financial Management Association (www.fma.org) ◆ Solution Matrix (www.soluionmatrix.com) ◆ American Institute of Certified Public Accountants (www.aicpa.org) ◆ Internet Public Library (www.ipl.org) ◆ Association for Financial Professionals (www.afponline.org) ◆ Ohio State Fisher College of Business (www.fisher.osu.edu/fin/journal/ofsites.htm)
Marketing associations	◆ American Marketing Association (www.marketingpower.com) ◆ Direct Marketing Association (www.the-dma.org) ◆ Marketing General Inc. (www.marketinggeneral.com) ◆ Produce Marketing Association (www.pma.com) ◆ Business Marketing Association (www.marketing.org) ◆ eMarketing Association (www.emarketingassociation.com)

STEP 3

Many factors influence the validity of data collection, and some factors can cause more harm than others. These factors include

◆ biased selection of respondents (for example, selecting employees from one area because you know they will participate)

◆ poor instrument creation

◆ the Hawthorne effect—being selected makes participants behave better

◆ respondent bias, whereby respondents want to influence you to do what they want done.

One other factor is worth noting: lack of contrary data collection. Typically there is some form of unconscious motivation or intention that will shape the questions we ask to create the outcomes we believe will be the case. To avoid this, it is important to ask for contrary data collection or to gather information from a view that is different from your own.

Being aware of potential validity and reliability problems is the first step in controlling them. As you move toward data analysis, identify potential problems that may have occurred as you collected the data. Knowing where your data are vulnerable and admitting it tends to stop arguments or disagreements when gaining commitment to your tactics. Table 3.5 identifies potential quality problems and explains how to avoid them.

TABLE 3.5

Methods for Controlling Data Quality

Quality Problem	How to Avoid the Problem
Lack of adequate experimental control	If modeling, testing, or some form of experimental design is part of the data gathering, it's important to ensure that the experiment has controls in place. These controls should not be manipulated. There must be specific timeframes, protocols for how and when groups are measured, clear guidelines on the extent to which the variable will be manipulated by the research, and random assignment of individuals to their experiment groups.

Table 3.5, continued

Quality Problem	How to Avoid the Problem
Inappropriate sample sizes	An incorrect sample size is often used, either because it is difficult to get the required number of responses or because there is not enough time to gather them. Conclusions can be incorrectly formulated because the sample size was too small to identify differences. It is best to choose the methods of data collection based on your sample size. Suggested sample sizes and data collection methods can be accessed through the Websites listed in this step.
Failure to see other solutions	While collecting and analyzing the data, it is important to keep an open mind and track other opportunities with vigilance. Oftentimes the analysis of one set of data will lead you to other information that you had not planned to collect. To make sure you have collected the right information, you must be willing to explore all "information avenues."
Failure to preserve data	Preserve the original data so that further or independent data analysis can be done, if desired. Keep all data, electronic or paper-based, until you have completed the strategic plan. If questions arise, you may need the raw data to support a conclusion, decision, or recommendation.
Misclassification or inaccurate structuring of the data	Precoding data collection forms for surveys and interviews can help in later data analysis problems. This allows the data to be structured (and thereby entered) correctly.
Poorly developed instruments	Instruments (interviews, surveys, observation forms) that are poorly developed will create quality issues. If the respondent is unsure what to do or has several choices, the data will be a comparison of apples and oranges and thereby invalid.
Lack of confidentiality	Ensuring that sensitive data are collected confidentially and maintained in the same manner is key to others believing in the data and their truth. If specific information is attributed to a person or a group, you run the risk of undermining your credibility and that of your plan.

◆ ◆ ◆

With the pertinent data in hand, the strategic planning group is ready to begin its analysis. That is the work of Step 4.

NOTES

_____

_____

_____

_____

_____

_____

_____

_____

_____

_____

_____

_____

_____

_____

_____

_____

_____

_____

_____

_____

_____

_____

Analyzing the Collected Data

OVERVIEW

Coding and sorting data

Analyzing data

Identifying key findings, conclusions, and recommendations

Validating your findings

Reporting findings and gaining commitment

Data analysis is the examination of information to arrive at a finding or discovery. Two primary methods are used to analyze data when developing a strategic plan: thematic analysis and quantitative analysis.

In *thematic analysis,* data are grouped or classified by specific content areas related to the strategic plan. This method helps you identify trends and validate similarities across the data. Data gathered through interviews and background research are typically analyzed using thematic analysis.

In *quantitative analysis,* data are assigned numbers and viewed statistically. Percentages, counts, comparisons, and mathematical calculations are performed and compiled to create findings. Although this type of analysis is most often used with surveys, it also can be used with data gleaned from interviews, focus groups, and other forms of data gathering.

In this step we'll cover the framework and tools you'll use to analyze the information you collected in Step 3. The text and the tools here will help you identify trends in your data that indicate the tactics that should be included in the strategic plan. They also will help

you control bias as much as possible and keep data distortion resulting from subjective information to a minimum. Specifically, this step
covers the following topics:

◆ coding and sorting your collected data

◆ organizing data for coding

◆ completing calculations

◆ analyzing data

◆ examining data to identify key findings, conclusions, and
   recommendations

◆ validating the findings

◆ reporting findings and gaining commitment.

As in our discussions of the first three steps, let's look first at a
couple of case examples.

Case Examples: Analyzing Data

These two case examples demonstrate how data analysis is used as
the basis for a strategic plan.

Learning from the Data

Tarlow Technologies is a three-year-old organization that develops
software. The HR group is new to the organization, and to align itself more strategically with management, the group decided to develop an HR strategic plan. Because all of the group members were
new to the company, they knew little about Tarlow's customer base,
products, or services. The strategy development process was a good
opportunity for the group to learn more about the organization and
to define how HR would operate during the next 18 months.

Because the company is small, the HR charter was to educate
both employees and customers. HR worked with marketing to gather
preexisting market research data about the customer base, the company's learning needs, and other relevant information. HR also conducted interviews with management and did background research to
identify how best-in-class companies provided learning product development and delivery to both customers and employees.

The group used thematic analysis to identify the major customer, business, learning, and finance trends in the information it gathered, and was able to determine which of those trends the strategic plan should address. The group identified how the trends aligned with the information gathered during the business scan conducted in Step 2.

By organizing and presenting the underlying facts logically, the HR group not only gained buy-in to the next step in developing the strategic plan, but also generated a brainstorming session that resulted in the HR group being seen as a strategic partner in delivering customer products and generating revenue for the company.

Bubbles Bursts into Data Analysis— And Its Strategy Pops Up

Bubbles is a retail store aimed at the children and teens market. It's enjoyed substantial growth through numerous bricks-and-mortar outlets across the country and now is positioning itself to expand internationally and through the Internet. To ensure that this expansion is re-addressed in its mission and that the strategy is on track, the strategy planning group has amassed a great deal of information. These data include financial information, industry comparisons, global and country analyses, and feedback from customers and suppliers. Early on in the data collection process, planners realized that the data from various sources would have to be cross-compared. A system for data coding was established and the files were entered in the database so that customer and supplier feedback could be compared. A pivot table (see the glossary for a definition) also was used to compare the children's wear cycles and growth in various countries. As a result of all this analysis, Bubbles discerned customer and supplier levels of satisfaction and identified the countries into which they would expand first.

Coding and Sorting Data

Your first step in data analysis is to identify how the data relate to the strategic plan and its corresponding outcomes, goals, and objectives. If you use the outcomes expected from the strategic plan and code the data components by outcome, your analysis will go more quickly. Coding your data as you do your interviews or research lets you build a data audit trail so that, as findings, conclusions, and recommendations are developed, you can trace them back to the original data on which you based them.

Coding can be completed in two ways: by strategy-related outcome or by the specific topic to which the data apply in the strategic plan. As you gather or review the data from your research, record the category code for each component in the margin or data file; for example, each data component related to risk and risk mitigation would be coded "RM."

Survey responses and notes from interviews, focus groups, and background research all can be coded (see Step 3). The sample interview guide (example 3.2) indicates how coding can be done by identifying the purpose of or the rationale for each question. The common categories for this type of research are

- ◆ *mission:* the organization's fundamental purpose or reason for existence
- ◆ *key challenges and business drivers:* the significant trials and barriers (key challenges) to meeting the internal and external forces (business drivers) that affect the organization as a whole (for example, the economy, public perception, international situation, and competition)
- ◆ *strategic outcome:* what you hope will happen as a result
- ◆ *risk and risk mitigation:* the potential undesired consequences of implementing the strategy's tactics, programs, and services, and how best to avoid those consequences
- ◆ *tactics:* the detailed information on tasks, timeframe, resource requirements, and budget requirements for the methods and approaches used to achieve the mission

- *metrics:* measurements that gauge the strategy's performance and track progress on its goals, objectives, and mission
- *resources:* the human, financial, and other assets needed to support the tactics and meet (or exceed) the desired outcomes.

Worksheet 4.1 demonstrates the use of coding to expedite the data analysis process for research findings.

Example 4.1 illustrates coding by objective. The first column identifies the objectives of the research. The middle column lists the code used for each objective. Column 3 lists the findings of the pertinent data, both qualitative and quantitative. Common data codes other than those indicating a theme are defined in example 4.2.

Organizing Data for Coding

It's helpful if you can be methodical in organizing your data for coding, as illustrated in examples 4.1 and 4.2. Having a system for organizing your data helps identify categories, patterns, themes, and logical relationships among the various data groups. It also creates an opportunity to ask additional questions about your data.

If you're working with a group, it's helpful to set up a three-column system on flipchart paper to organize the data. The three columns are

1. *preexisting categories,* such as outcomes, business drivers, mission, and so forth
2. *data codes*, as described in example 4.2
3. *parking lot,* where anything that doesn't fit in the first column can be placed temporarily.

When you've organized the data into the categories you identified earlier, reexamine the data and identify new themes or categories for the parking lot data. As you categorize that "new data," create another three-column chart, making notes about your hypothesis and the reasoning behind the new theme(s).

WORKSHEET 4.1

Thematic Analysis for Examining Data and Identifying Findings

Instructions: Topics typically included in a strategic plan are listed in column 1. In column 2, write the source of relevant data you have collected. If the source is an interview or survey question, note the question number. In column 3, record the data gathered. In column 4, describe what you have learned from the data—your key findings. The first topic has been completed as an example.

Analysis Topic	Related Source or Question	Data Gathered	Findings Related to Data
Mission	• *Interview Q1* • *Survey Q6*	• *Create and maintain a knowledge bank for the organization* • *Build leadership skills and talent* • *Enhance skills that directly contribute to sales*	*Responses for our mission varied by level of position within company, but the overall theme is that we are responsible for creating and maintaining skills and knowledge critical to the organization.*
Key challenges and business drivers			
Purpose of training and related key initiatives			

Risk and risk mitigation			
Metrics			
Tactics			
Resources			
Other:			

EXAMPLE 4.1

Data Coding by Objective

Objective	Code	Data Related to Code
To discover our organization's customer issues that our products, programs, and services should address	Customer issues	• Expectations are different in a deregulated environment. Customers are knowledge able and expect staff to be so. We do not have information regarding customers that will support us going forward. We are unable to articulate why customers should use our products and services rather than the competition's. • Seventy-three percent of our customers said they knew more bout new products than did the employees answering phones in the call center. • Thirty-two percent of our custom-ers said that they were considering moving to a competitor.
To identify how we compare to our competition	Competition	We do not understand who our competition is.
To determine how to align with technology to improve employee performance within the organization	Technology	• We do not have the technology to support the infrastructure, processes, and procedures • Fifty-one percent of our employees identified the lack of technology to support their job functions as a very likely source of poor performance.
To identify critical gaps in employee performance	Lack of internatl ability	• Current staff do not have the skills to compete in a deregulated environment. Staff are not creative or dynamic and do not think as they would in a deregulated environment. Customers are knowledgeable and expect staff to be as well.

This type of organization helps you identify various relationships that exist among the data and, ultimately, will lead you to your findings, conclusions, and recommendations. A word of caution, however: Because bias makes it easy to see themes and relationships where they really don't exist, have others who are not as involved in the data analysis play the devil's advocate.

If a group is coding data, share the coding and data with a peer or group of peers to see the data similarities. If agreed to, this provides a degree of reliability in your coding process. If the data coding is a group event, beware of how agreement was reached. Did a dominant player with seniority or strong feelings/opinions about the data or the ultimate outcome influence the ultimate agreement? This is called the *falsification principle*. In other words, the

EXAMPLE 4.2

Nonthematic Data Codes

Code	Meaning	Explanation
I	Impression	The analyzer's impression; implied but not necessarily stated directly in the data or interview
Q	Quote	Directly stated in the data or a quote from the interview
F	Frequent	Repeatedly found in the data
S	Sporadic	Found in the data once or twice
Q#	Number of the question to which data are related	If the data were found in a response to another question, note the question number it relates to next to the data. For example, if information related to Mission (Q1) is found in Other (Q19), note the question number (Q1) beside the information you document in Q19.
P#	Letter of the probe related to a specific question	Note the probe letter if the information was provided as a response to a particular probe.

finding is untrue and not based on facts—it's the result of opinions or influence.

There are various resources available to assist you in your research and in coding the data you collect. These resources are listed with a brief description in tool 4.1.

Completing Calculations

Survey feedback usually is reported using descriptive statistics—numbers that summarize how items were answered on the questionnaire. Here are typical descriptive statistics for surveys:

◆ Frequency, or how many responses were provided for each item (for example, 6 of 20 for response *a*, four of 20 for *b*, 10 of 20 for *c*)

TOOL 4.1

Data and Coding Resources

Resource	Description
Action Research Resources (www.scu.edu.au/schools/g cm/ar/arp/grounded.html)	Presents discussions of and processes for coding, sorting, and notetaking
Knowledgestorm (www .knowledgestorm.com)	Offers data sites for specific research needs
Blue Claw Database Design (www.blueclaw-db.com)	Offers examples of Microsoft Access studies
Kerlins.net (www.kerlins.net)	Provides specific information for qualitative research as well as an in-depth bibliography
Ask.com search engine (www.ask.com)	Provides several search tools that enable you to determine what sites are most beneficial before you access them
University of Pennsylvania (www.wharton.upenn.edu)	Includes information on new theories and research methods

◆ Percentage, which converts frequency to a proportion by dividing the number of specific responses by the total number of responses, and then multiplying by 100 (for example, 30 percent for response *a*, 20 percent for *b*, 50 percent for *c*)

◆ Cumulative frequency, which identifies how many respondents selected a specific number on a Likert scale (for example, 20 of 100 gave a ranking of 3, on a scale of 1 to 5, for the level of technical sophistication of our product support courseware)

◆ Cumulative percentage, which simply converts cumulative frequency to a proportion (for example, 20 percent gave a ranking of 3, on a scale of 1 to 5, for the level of technical sophistication of our product support courseware)

◆ Averages by which data are represented as a "typical value":

• *Mean* is most commonly thought of as an average, and it represents all the data values added together and divided by the number of items (for example, 12 + 10 + 10 + 12 = 44, and 44 divided by 4 = 11, so 11 is the average of the four numbers. (The mean is not the same as the median.)

• *Median*, the middle or midpoint of a group of numbers put in order. For example, in the nine-number group 2, 4, 5, 8, 9, 19, 20, 21, 22, the fifth number (9) is the median. If the group of numbers is even, take the two numbers that are in the middle and average them to produce the median—that is, the median of the even-numbered group 2, 4, 5, 8, 9, 19, 20, 21 would be 8.5.

> **POINTER**
> Consistent data analysis used by all members responsible for the analysis ensures that the results will be complete and accurate.

• *Mode*, which is typically the least used of the averages, is the most repeated number in the group. For example, in a group of leadership scores there were the following results: 70, 82, 90, 90, 86, 82, 82, 90, 85, 82, 70, 61, 82, 93, 96. The mode is 82.

◆ Ranges of variation, which let you know how reliable your data are. The most common way a variation in data is described is through the *standard deviation*—the square root of the variance. The *variance* is found by subtracting the average from each data item. In most cases, there will be as many negative (items below the average) as positive (items above the average) numbers. Generally 68.3 percent of the data will be within 1 standard deviation of the mean.

Analyzing Data

When all people responsible for analyzing the data collected are using consistent analysis methods, the results will be complete and accurate. Consistency also identifies the data tests that will be performed and how findings will be addressed and tested. Tool 4.2 lists and describes the steps to completing the data analysis process.

Examining Data to Identify Key Findings, Conclusions, and Recommendations

Deciding what your findings are basically is a matter of interpreting the data. But you must go beyond the descriptive data or interview notes and the categories and themes that you developed in creating the data-gathering tools to determine the significance of what you found, to offer explanations, to draw conclusions, to extrapolate ideas, to make inferences, or to create linkages—in short, to attach meaning to the data. We've exemplified how to complete a finding in the first item on worksheet 4.1, Mission.

To arrive at a finding, first confirm that what you say is a "finding" truly is one by validating it against other data. For example, let's say that in interviews you conducted with customers, most indicated that they use some form of Web support to identify product features and benefits. You can validate this as a finding by

TOOL 4.2

Steps in the Data Analysis Process

Process Step	Step Description
1. Identify the scope of the analysis	Using the objectives and goals for the strategic plan, identify how these data are relevant to the plan itself.
2. Ensure the reliability of the raw data	Review the data and the collection process to ensure it was carried out in a way that it is pure, and that there is no bias or manipulation of the data.
3. Extract the data	Extract the data and verify its integrity, completeness, and relevancy.
4. Import or input data to a data analysis tool or worksheets	Put the data into some sort of database reporting tool (or a manual worksheet), and ensure that the data have been input/imported correctly. The data fields should match the data that has been imported in them (for example, Age: 35, not ABCD).
5. Profile the data	Run an initial database report to ensure that no data have been omitted and that the data are relevant (for example, an employee's name is incorrectly listed as John instead of Joan, or the department to which an employee is assigned is wrong).
6. Analyze the data from the database	Analyze the data to identify evidence, conclusions, and first-level findings.
7. Report the data	Identify the type of report you will use to report the data and the findings associated with them.
8. Document the findings	Document the findings and provide evidence for those findings in the form of reports, spreadsheets, flowcharts, results of observations, and so forth.

STEP

4

comparing it with your best-practices research to determine if this is a growing consumer trend.

When you've identified all of your findings, choose those you consider key. You identify *key findings* by isolating specific variables that you think are important for the development of the strategy, and then determining if there are any interdependencies. In other words, *if we* [something], *then* [something else] *will occur*—and it's the "something else" that we want. Here's an example: *If we* develop a strong management program that emphasizes leadership, *then we* will create a pool of senior-level managers within our organization. When you've identified your key findings, add them to column 4 of worksheet 4.1.

Conclusions in this context are your interpretations of key findings—what the findings mean relative to the strategic plan. You may decide that before you interpret the meaning of a key finding, you need to sort the data differently. You may need to sort them by various demographic groups and determine if the finding is true across those groups or if it pertains to just one or two groups. Let's say a key finding is that employee turnover is very high. As a result of this finding, the HR manager wants to know what role HR can play in decreasing turnover or increasing retention. The manager re-sorts the turnover information, and the re-sorting reveals that the majority of turnover is in the information systems department. If the department's employees are leaving for higher-paying jobs and shorter hours, HR may not be a key player in this turnover. On the other hand, if employee dissatisfaction or managerial problems are prompting the departures, HR may play a critical role and the conclusion may be that further investigation is needed about what that role should be.

Recommendations are derived from the findings and the conclusions, and they form the basis for the tactical plan in the strategic plan. Using the turnover example above, the recommendation for the strategic plan may be to work with other HR business partners to identify the products and services HR can provide to information systems managers to help reduce turnover in that department.

Example 4.3 illustrates how you track the conclusions and recommendations with the findings that support them. It is possible that in some future time, there will be questions about why you chose to implement specific tactics. The examples in this table were created from the data in example 4.1.

Validating the Findings

Validating the findings means determining if they are accurate, stable, and repeatable. Can you trust the numbers? Is the information being used as it was intended in the instrumentation, or have you altered the numerical findings so they lead you to a mistaken conclusion? For example, if 90 percent of those responding to a survey indicated they prefer taking computer training for "some subjects," you can't claim the finding that respondents prefer computer training for *all* subjects.

Here's an example of findings that validate each other: If the organizational findings indicate that sales are falling and the organization is losing customers, and the survey data indicate that your respondents feel they're unable to compete for sales effectively because they don't have accurate competitor information, then you can begin to build a cause-and-effect scenario. The organizational findings (reduced sales, customer flight) validate the survey findings (competitive inequity, lack of information), and vice versa.

There are several testing methods you can use to ensure that the findings are supportable and relevant to the data. Tool 4.3 provides examples and descriptions of the four most common methods for testing data findings.

It's also helpful to validate relationships between the data and the strategic outcomes. You can validate these relationships by asking yourself or the planning team the following five questions:

1. How does (or doesn't) this finding relate to the current strategic outcomes?
2. What more do I need to know about this finding and its relationship to the outcomes?

EXAMPLE 4.3

Relating Conclusions and Recommendations to Key Findings

Conclusion	Supporting Key Findings
1. As a result of deregulation, our product line and competition changed. We are now in an environment where our customers have more knowledge about us than we have about them and about how we can be of assistance to them.	◆ Expectations are different in a deregulated environment. Customers are knowledgeable and expect staff to be so. We do not have information regarding customers that will support us going forward. We are unable to articulate why customers should use our products and services rather than the competition's. ◆ Seventy-three percent of our customers said they knew more about new products than did the employees answering our call center phones. ◆ Thirty-two percent of our customers said they were considering moving to a competitor.
2. We do not have information readily available about our competition and therefore do not understand how we differ or what we do that is similar.	◆ We do not understand who our competition is.
3. Performance problems are compounded by the lack of technology to support our infrastructure, processes, and procedures.	◆ We do not have the technology to support the infrastructure, processes, and procedures. ◆ Fifty-one percent of our employees identified the lack of technology to support their job functions as a very likely source of poor performance.

Recommendation	Supporting Key Findings
1. The organization needs to provide course-ware and job aids that assist employees in understanding the customer, our product line, and how to assess customer needs and match products to them.	◆ Expectations are different in a deregulated environment. Customers are knowledgeable and expect staff to be so. We do not have information regarding customers that will support us going forward. We are unable to articulate why customers should use our products and services rather than the competition's. ◆ Seventy-three percent of our customers said they knew more about new products than did the employees answering our call center phones. ◆ Thirty-two percent of our customers said that they were considering moving to a competitor.
2. The organization needs to partner with marketing or another group and work on a competitive study so job aids and information about our competition can be built into our training products and services.	◆ We do not understand who our competition is.
3. The organization needs to partner with information services to create an electronic performance support system that will provide necessary information, processes, and procedures to employees on their desktops.	◆ We do not have technology to support the infrastructure, processes, and procedures. ◆ Fifty-one percent of our employees identified the lack of technology to support their job functions as a very likely source of poor performance.

TOOL 4.3

Methods for Testing the Validity of Your Findings

Test Method	Descriptions
Initial thesis	In data analysis you sometimes see an initial explanation that has never been considered before. It's possible this thesis will result in an emerging opportunity to change or tweak the outcomes, goals, and objectives of the strategic plan and so will vastly affect your organization as a whole over the long term. It is probable that you'll find that more research is needed to prove or disprove that this thesis is the right path to travel.
Cause and effect	In data analysis, you often can identify what the core or original problem is, but you are unsure what might be the ultimate source of that problem. For example, cost of inventory is rising in the organization. There could be many "causes"—perhaps storage cost is rising because of higher rental or lease rates, the inventory product itself is rising, product cost is lowering but is offset by the rising storage cost. It's important to look at all the variables that may affect the rise in the cost of inventory before changing a factor. Perhaps you are increasing inventory because you know in the next season the product will no longer be available or will be more costly. This is why looking closely at causes and effects in data analysis can ensure you don't jump to the wrong conclusions or make poor decisions.
Triangulation	When a variety of data sources all have the same results, it can lead to a strong finding. For example, if your customers are saying that the salespeople are ill-trained on the product and cannot speak to the benefits and disadvantages, and the business partners say that product training for your organization is poor, and the salesforce says product training is either poor or nonexistent, then product training most likely is something your organization needs to work on. If different data methods—perhaps a literature search, interviews, and a survey—resulted in the same findings, this is triangulation.
Multiple factors	In this test you are looking at the same effect in multiple factors—for example, a rise in price, falling customer satisfaction with the product, lower organizational revenue, decreased competitive advantage, and less ability to market actively to new prospects. In other words, the evidence shows that one factor (price increase) influenced multiple other factors in the organization; it did not affect only one component.

TOOL 4.4

Additional Questions for Validating Findings

Question	Rationale
Do you have any questions about the findings? Are the findings understandable?	To reveal resistance to or problems with the findings early on so that they can be resolved
Is there any finding here that you think we need to know more about before proceeding?	To uncover any missing information about new programs or factors that might influence the findings
Did any of the findings surprise you?	To validate the information (normally the findings won't surprise anyone, but if they do, the audit trail of source and response may enable others to see why the findings are what they are)

3. Why is more information needed to validate this finding's relationship to the strategic outcomes?

4. How will I use this finding in relation to the strategic plan?

5. Is there another reason that this finding is related to the outcomes?

After validating the findings against the strategy, ask yourself or the team some additional questions. You'll find these questions and the rationale behind asking them in tool 4.4.

Finally, if your organization uses a "balanced scorecard" (as in Norton/Kaplan's Balanced Scorecard) for strategic planning or for performance measurement, then it may be helpful to use this scorecard to validate your findings by identifying the cause and effect through the four levels. Figure 4.1 identifies the cause and effect of the findings in learning, business, customer, and financial aspects, and how they relate to each other. By using this cause-and-effect process to relate your findings, you'll shorten the process to develop a balanced scorecard for your strategic plan. This cause-and-effect diagram supports strategic plan scorecard development and

FIGURE 4.1

Cause-and-Effect Findings Diagram for a Balanced Scorecard Strategic Plan

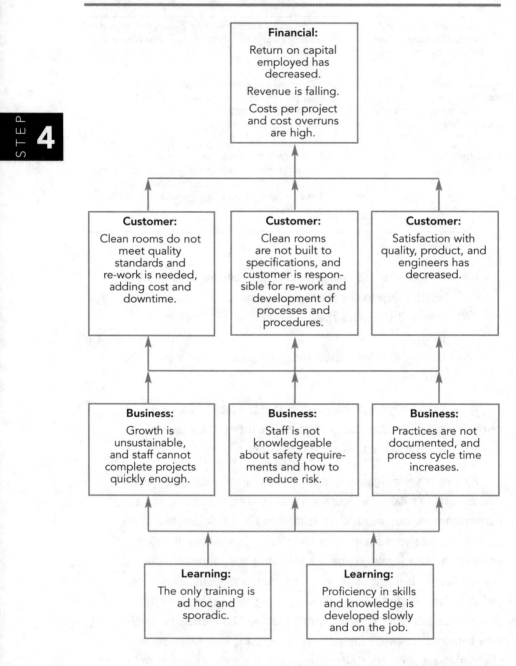

helps managers see that not all business issues would be affected by one change. For example, growth is unsustainable, but senior management would need to assign other resources to resolve this larger problem.

When you've tested and validated your findings, you're ready to document them for others to see and debate.

Reporting Findings and Gaining Commitment

The report on the findings should be concise and to the point. Aim for a three- to five-page report at most, although more people are likely to read your report if it is only two pages long. With this in mind, an outline for a findings report is provided in Tool 4.5. The content areas of the report are listed and described in columns 1 and 2, and there is space in the final column for your notes as you prepare the outline for your report.

The report should be distributed to stakeholders, business partners, sponsors, members of the strategic planning group, and, if appropriate, to participating customers. You probably will want to have a much shorter version with just the key findings and conclusions for those who participated in the information gathering. This could be housed on a Website and referred to when you ask for their assistance in gaining commitment. It's important that all parties who see any portion of this report understand that it's the data analysis report and *not* the strategic plan!

As part of the process of gaining commitment, you should solicit specific information from your stakeholders, business partners, sponsors, and others who will assist you in implementing the strategy. An effective method to solicit this information and encourage commitment is to ask them questions about the reported findings and conclusions. Tool 4.6 lists some questions to use in this process and the rationale for asking these questions to gain commitment.

TOOL 4.5

Components of a Data Analysis Findings Report

Section of Report	Description	Your Notes
Executive summary	Brief (and interesting) summary of the report's highlights	
Purpose of report	How this report supports the strategic plan development, or how the data in this report will be used	
Data collection process	Steps (and description) of the data collection and analysis process used	
Summarized data	Data summarized for report	
Significant or key findings	List of key findings	
Recommendations for consideration	Recommendations for tactics for consideration, organized by strategic outcome	
Acknowledgments	Recognition of those people involved in the data collection process and those who participated	
Listing of data sources	List of the data sources and methods used to gather the data	

It's important to use influence when gaining commitment and agreement to the recommendations made for the strategic plan. Although influencing tends to be a complex and often subtle process, there are some specific tactics you can use. First, be logical rather than emotional in your approach. Use facts and evidence to build a persuasive case. Ask questions to get input on how this type of

TOOL 4.6

Questions for Gaining Commitment

Question	Rationale
Are there other groups with whom we should share these findings?	To build outreach for the strategy and get others involved in how the organization plans to progress; it's also an important beginning in building additional partnerships if needed.
Does anyone have questions about the conclusions and recommendations?	To reveal any resistance and gain commitment to going forward with the strategic plan.
If the organization begins to move forward with these recommendations, do you feel we would be acting in the best interests of our company, customers, and employees?	To gauge support for the recommendations and uncover any further resistance to the organization's moving forward.
Are there others we should include in our planning sessions as we move forward?	To open an opportunity for others to get involved and partner with you; if you have a specific resource need, the question can be changed to: Is [a certain employee] available to work with us as we move forward?
Are there any objections to our moving forward in the development of the strategic plan at this point?	To bring closure to the validation meeting and announce that the organization is moving forward. There usually are questions about when you expect the plan to be finished and if there will be another review. (Typically, you are about two to three weeks from wrapping up the plan, and normally you will want an additional meeting with your stakeholders and business partners to gain their final commitment to go ahead with the tactics and resource allocation.)

data will be used in the future. Remember, the ultimate result is to build a strategic plan that inspires others to make a move in the strategic direction. Other questions to ask yourself as you begin to build your case include

1. What are the major areas of agreement in the data findings?

2. What are the main differences in people's perceptions of the data findings, conclusions, and recommendations?
3. What aspects of the findings clearly relate to the outcomes as we have defined them?
4. What aspects of the findings, conclusions, and recommendations have potential for exciting others to participate in the strategic direction of the organization?

When you meet with various groups, you can enlist their help to gain commitment across the organization. During advocate interviews you might ask the questions outlined in tool 4.6.

◆ ◆ ◆

Much of the tedious work of planning is behind you now. The findings, conclusions, and recommendations that have resulted from your data collection will be the foundation for the remainder of the work. Your next step is to develop your mission statement, and that will be discussed in Step 5.

NOTES

Stating Mission, Vision, and Values

OVERVIEW

Defining mission, vision, and values

Creating a mission statement and objectives

Writing a clear vision statement

Stating the organization's values and desired behaviors

When a marketing professor interviewed various successful chief executive officers, he asked them what they saw as the most valuable underused asset in business. Their first response was human resources; the second was the mission statement. In further discussions, the CEOs talked about how most organizations write a mission statement and then use it only occasionally in new employee orientations, sales meetings, and the like. All too often it is seen as "just a statement about the organization." We believe, instead, that the mission statement should be an introduction to all who touch the organization—customers, business partners, employees, and even the general public. This statement should inspire all of these groups to support and work with the organization to carry out its mission.

A mission statement should be a brief, clear declaration about why your organization exists. It gives the organization a framework for devising the services, products, and programs it will offer its customers in fulfillment of that mission. But it's much more than a framework for the rest of the organization's strategy. Table 5.1 lists the many ways that a mission statement can be used.

When a marketing professor interviewed various successful CEOs, he asked what they saw as the most valuable underused asset in business. First answer: human resources; second: the mission statement.

In this step we'll explain the process and give you tools for creating mission, vision, and values statements for your organization. As you develop specific tactics and action plans in crafting a strategy, the mission statement helps ensure that what you're planning actually will deliver what the organization needs. The vision statement will define where your organization is going in the future. The values statements will guide how your executives, managers, and employees behave in the present and the future. Specifically, this step focuses on

- ◆ defining mission, vision, and values statements
- ◆ setting an agenda for creating mission, vision, and values statements
- ◆ reviewing key findings from the analysis completed in Step 4
- ◆ creating a mission statement and objectives
- ◆ creating a vision statement
- ◆ creating values statements.

First we'll look at the details of three brief case studies to see how these statements affected the organizations involved.

Case Examples: Mission and Vision Statements

These case examples demonstrate how organizations have developed and used mission, vision, and values statements in their strategic planning.

Ryan's Revises Its Mission and Vision to Match Its Expansion

Ryan's Trains began as a store selling model trains, but it's become much more. It now sells model trains, toy trains, mementos, and

TABLE 5.1

Uses of a Mission Statement

Use	Definition of Use
To gain commitment	The mission statement can be used or presented to gain buy-in to the organization's function, customer base, processes, and purpose.
To serve as a communication device	The mission statement can be used to communicate with employees, customers, competitors, business partners, stakeholders, sponsors, and others in the larger community about what the organization does; how and why it does it; and to whom it offers its products, services, and programs.
To serve as a marketing slogan	Because the mission statement is concise, it can be used in materials, Webpages, and other communication devices to market the organization's services, programs, and products.
To set expectations	The mission statement can be used to describe the role the organization will play in the community and the industry, and to clarify what it expects from those who work with it.
To initiate dialogue	The mission statement can be used to open a conversation with others or to introduce the organization to customers, employees, business partners, and people who may not know of its services, products, and programs.

collectibles. Ryan's recently began a franchise system and purchased an old train station that's being renovated into a train amusement park.

When the strategic planners began reviewing the existing plan, they suggested that the previous mission ("Ryan's Trains provides children and adults with high-quality train models at the most affordable price and with the highest customer care") was outdated. After a brainstorming session, the new mission statement became "Ryan's Trains offers a variety of high-quality opportunities for families to engage in activities that support learning about trains and increase interest in the train industry."

The values statements that were original to Ryan's were still valid, and the planning group updated the vision to reflect the three- to four-year plan for the company.

Crafting a Vision Statement That Reveals the Future

Endicott Services is a consulting firm that supplies project personnel for companies worldwide. The firm's mission statement reads, "We provide high-quality individuals internationally to lead and/or support projects that increase productivity, profitability, and the quality of our clients' organizations."

Endicott's strategic planning group agreed that the mission statement still reflects the company's business and the environment in which it works. The group also reviewed and approved these values statements:

- We will represent Endicott in all our client and community relationships by behaving ethically.
- We will be fiscally responsible in our actions, both for our client and our company.
- We will be creative and innovative when attacking project issues and problems.
- We will manage change by respecting the scope, schedule, and budget of the project.
- We will demand two-way communications to solve all problems.
- We will be ready and able to face and manage any and all conflicts.

The vision statement, however, did need to reflect a new direction for the company. Previously, the vision statement had been directed at developing a comprehensive training program for new employees so that they readily could act as Endicott representatives on any client's project. The new vision written by the planning group is, "Within three years, Endicott Services will develop a new income stream by devising a leading-edge project management system that will help our clients manage project tasks, cost, timeframe, people, and scope."

Writing Statements That Garner Support for Good Causes

ACT (Animals, Care and Treatment) is a not-for-profit organization that cares for mistreated animals and places them in new homes where they will be loved and well cared for. The organization realized during fundraising that well-defined mission, vision, and values statements would help it raise much-needed funds from individuals, corporations, and foundations.

At an off-site planning retreat, the group dedicated part of its agenda time to writing its new mission, vision, and values statements. The group brainstormed, reviewed other organizations' statements, and used criteria to evaluate the worth of the statements they wrote.

When their statements were finished, everyone at the retreat was surprised by how much they benefited fundraising, marketing, and volunteer recruiting efforts, and their work with veterinarians who contributed care pro bono. Here are the statements written by ACT's strategy planners:

Mission: Our mission is to provide top-quality care to animals that have been mistreated and that demand our love and attention to transform them into functioning pets for adoption into loving homes.

Vision: Our vision is, within three years, to develop a 200-patient facility, and to place more than 2,000 pets in good-quality homes.

Values: Our values are to respect animal rights, promote animal well-being, and develop relationships between animals and humans for the benefit of both parties.

Defining Mission, Vision, and Values Statements

Although mission, vision, and values statements often are grouped together, each of them contributes something different to the organization in executing the strategy.

The mission statement is concise and direct. It specifies the reason for the organization and what sets it apart from the competition and other similar organizations. It should address the following issues:

1. the reason the organization exists
2. who the organization serves (the main customer or client)
3. the value of the organization to others.

The mission statement rarely needs updating unless there is a major change or reorganization in the company—a product expansion, shifting customer demographics, or operational upheaval.

The vision statement, on the other hand, tends to remain current for only two to four years. It describes where the organization is going or how its future is imagined, and tends to be more idealistic and inspirational than does the mission statement. It should address these issues:

1. the future direction of the company
2. a measurement (time required/allotted, degree/percentage of change, increase/decrease in dollars) that defines the future change
3. how the organization will look when the strategy has been met
4. the organization's message in realistic and credible terms consistent with its mission and values.

Values statements identify the traits, behaviors, or qualities that typify the organization's actions. The values statements should

1. define how employees, managers, and executives behave
2. reflect the values of management, the board of directors/trustees, and any others who ultimately dictate the organization's actions

3. be the values of those employed by the organization
4. define the foundation of the organizational culture (how all members will walk the talk)
5. drive company decisions.

Table 5.2 illustrates how the mission, vision, and values statements affect relationships between the company and its customers, the company and its business partners, between product development and execution, and between the present and the future. Column 1 gives examples of the relationships, and columns 2, 3, and 4 identify how the mission, vision, and values affect those relationships.

Setting an Agenda for Creating the Mission, Vision, and Values Statements

It can be very productive for the strategic planning group to hold a brainstorming session to develop mission, vision, and values statements. The content of the agenda depends on your group's working relationships; how long members have been with the organization; and how much each member knows about the findings, conclusions, and recommendations arrived at in Step 4. Tool 5.1 contains three suggested agendas. The first column describes three planning group scenarios that indicate factors to consider in setting the duration and agenda for your next meeting. Choose the scenario that best describes your group's circumstances, and then consult the second column for agenda items and amounts of time to allot to each.

It may be advisable to have a representative from the HR department facilitate the brainstorming session or to hire a facilitator from outside the organization to do so. The facilitator must be unbiased about what the mission, vision, and values statements contain.

Reviewing Key Findings

If the strategic planning group was not intimately involved in analyzing the data, identifying conclusions, and creating recommendations, it's wise to review and process the findings with members be-

TABLE 5.2

How the Mission, Vision, and Values Statements Affect Entities Related to the Organization

Related Entity	What the Mission Statement Explains	What the Vision Statement Explains	What the Values Statements Explain
Customer	Why the organization exists, and who are the customers it serves	Where the organization is going, and what customers can expect in the future	How the organization interacts with customers, and what it values so that customers/prospects can evaluate if the organization is in sync with its own values
Prospective customer	Why the organization exists, who are the customers served, and what types of products are offered	The future direction of the organization	How the organization interacts with customers, and what it values so that customers/prospects can evaluate if the organization is in sync with its own values
Employee	What makes the organization unique, the nature of the business, the identity of the customers, and what products and services are offered	What direction the organization is taking and why, what areas of specialization will be needed in the future, and what timeline does this future vision anticipate	The behaviors expected of those representing the organization
Business partner	What makes the organization unique, the nature of the business, the identity of the customers, and what products and services are offered	The organization's future direction and the anticipated timeline	The behaviors expected of those representing the organization

Public at-large	What makes the organization unique, the nature of the business, the identity of the customers, and what products and services are offered	The future direction of the organization	The behaviors expected of those representing the organization
Product	Product and service limitations identified for targeted customers	Product changes for the future, and the timeline for those changes	How the products and services will be created, offered, and supported; and the behaviors expected of those representing the organization
The present	Who the organization is today, and why it is who it is	Not applicable	What the organization expects from its strategies, people, and products; and the behaviors expected of those representing the organization
The future	Not applicable	Where the organization is going	What the organization expects from its strategies, people, and products; and the behaviors expected of those representing the organization

STEP

5

TOOL 5.1

Suggested Agendas for Creating Mission, Vision, and Values Statements

Group Scenario	Suggested Agenda Items and Timing
The group has not participated in the analysis and is either seeing the information from the data gathering or discussing it as a group for the first time. The group has little experience working together and group norms are unknown, so more time will be needed to build trust and a working relationship. Several new people have joined the group since the process began, and they need to be oriented. The mission, vision, and values may need to be updated or to be written from scratch.	Schedule a full-day meeting to ♦ orient the group to the process that is being followed (30 minutes) ♦ update the group on the status of the strategic plan (30 minutes) ♦ present the findings (45 minutes) ♦ facilitate processing of the findings, conclusions, and recommendations; and interpret what they mean to the mission, vision, and values statements (one to two hours) ♦ determine if the mission needs to be updated (30 minutes) ♦ if so, brainstorm its contents (30 to 60 minutes) ♦ determine if the values should be updated, and if so, discuss why and what needs to change (30 minutes) ♦ choose the contents for the vision and validate them against the findings (30 to 60 minutes) ♦ discuss next steps to be taken to complete the mission, vision, and values statements (30 minutes)
Various individuals or subgroups own parts of the strategy and will be responsible for building the tactics and identifying and prioritizing the resources. This session needs to refocus the group on the mission and look ahead so the rest of the steps can be completed.	Schedule a half-day meeting to ♦ determine if the mission needs to be updated (30 minutes) ♦ if so, brainstorm its contents (30 to 60 minutes) ♦ determine if the values should be updated, and if so, discuss why and what needs to change (30 minutes)

The group has previously shared in the analysis and interpretation of the data and is ready to create the mission statement. The mission, vision, and values may need to be updated.	◆ choose the contents for the vision and validate them against the findings (30 to 60 minutes) ◆ discuss next steps to be taken to complete the mission, vision, and values statements (30 minutes)
The group has a strong working relationship, forged over more than a year. Mapping of the business drivers and organization were successfully done and agreed on by all members. The group has shared in the analysis and interpretation of the data and is ready to write the mission statement. Group members are committed to building tactics and action plans and to determining resources together. It has been agreed that the mission and values are current and do not need to be updated.	Schedule a two-hour meeting to ◆ review the current mission and values and reconfirm that these do not need to be changed (15 minutes or less) ◆ choose the contents for the vision and validate them against the findings (30 to 60 minutes) ◆ discuss next steps to be taken to complete the values statements (30 minutes)

fore creating the mission statement and objectives. Processing these findings gives group members an opportunity to question the findings, understand the conclusions, and come to their own decisions about how the information gathered affects the strategic plan and the mission, vision, and values.

To prepare for the findings review, send everyone involved in creating the mission, vision, and values statements a copy of the key findings, conclusions, and recommendations and a key findings worksheet (worksheet 5.1). This worksheet was designed to help group members think about what the findings, conclusions, and recommendations mean in relation to creating the mission statement, objectives, and strategic plan. Each group member should complete the worksheet before the brainstorming meeting to generate thoughts and discussion items. Send an accompanying cover letter that explains how members should use the materials to prepare for the meeting.

If the group is large, you may want to break it into small groups for discussion and then come together for a final facilitation period. Regardless of group size, the following process will help facilitate the discussion:

◆ Using a flipchart, list the findings, conclusions, and recommendations that surprised members of the group. As you list these items, identify why the item was surprising:
  - Was it new information?
  - Is it contrary to what he or she previously thought?
  - If the employee is new to the group, is it different from what he or she has been accustomed to?
  - Is the item representative of a change in the organization, the culture, the customer group, the environment, or some other factor?
  - Is there comfort or discomfort in the surprise?
  - What may ease any discomfort (for example, more information)?
◆ With a list you've created beforehand (perhaps on a flipchart, a PowerPoint slide, or an overhead transparency), review the findings and identify the conclusions and recommendations that the group supports and is comfortable with.

WORKSHEET 5.1

Review of Key Findings

Findings Review Question	Your Thoughts
1. Were you surprised by any of the key findings, conclusions, or recommendations? If so, what was surprising to you, and why?	
2. Did any of the key findings, conclusions, or recommendations make you uncomfortable? If so, what about the information made you uncomfortable, and why?	
3. Which of the key findings, conclusions, or recommendations provided information that you think is crucial to include in some form in the strategic plan? Why is it important, or what is important about it?	
4. On what information do you think it important that specific groups, departments, or individuals act? Why do you think it is important that they specifically should be assigned to this information or finding?	
5. As a result of reviewing this information, what one thing above all others should the organization champion within the strategic plan, and why?	
6. What key information was conveyed to you when you reviewed the cause-and-effect diagram?	

◆ Identify the conclusions and recommendations that the group does not feel comfortable with. Probe to learn more:

- What is the discomfort?
- Will the discomfort affect their creating the mission statement or objectives and, if so, how?
- How can the group members become more comfortable—what do they need to do or know? (It's important to acknowledge the discomfort at this point, but also to determine if the discomfort is a show-stopper.)

When the group or subgroups have discussed the findings, use the following questions for a final discussion:

1. What information in the findings, conclusions, and recommendations do you think should influence the mission statement, and how?
2. Do the findings, conclusions, and recommendations influence what you think about the strategy's mission statement and objectives?
3. What information do you think is critical to include in the mission statement?
4. What information do you think is critical to include in the mission objectives?
5. What information should not be included at this time? Why?
6. What information should be provided to others for action, with the caveat that it is not something the organization is working on at this time?

Creating a Mission Statement

The mission statement should answer five questions:

1. Why does the organization exist? What is its value to its customers, its stakeholders, and its business partners?
2. Who is the organization's customer base? Is it a specific demographic group? Is it a group involved in a specific activity, such as skiing or teaching science?
3. What function(s) does the organization perform for its customers?

TOOL 5.2

Brainstorming Guidelines

1. Everyone should participate.

2. Don't evaluate your ideas—just get them out of your head and up on the flipchart or whiteboard. Speak whatever comes to you—don't hold back.

3. Don't evaluate others' ideas—it slows down the process and isn't productive.

4. There is no wrong answer or bad idea in a brainstorming session.

5. Piggybacking, or adding onto someone else's idea, is encouraged.

4. How does the organization do its work or fill its function(s)?

5. If the organization did not exist, what would be absent in the marketplace?

If the mission statement answers these questions, it will express the scope and direction of the organization's activities and form a basis for the decisions on objectives, tactics, and resources for the strategic plan. The mission statement also guides members of the strategic planning group in communicating what the organization does and why, and helps articulate why the organization can and cannot be involved in specific work.

Because much of this work is done in brainstorming sessions, we've included some useful brainstorming guidelines for you to share with the group. You'll find them in tool 5.2.

Example 5.1 offers some sample mission statements for your review. Share them with your group at the outset to "prime the pump" or reserve them for that time when the group gets stuck in writing its own statement.

Here are some key questions to ask as you brainstorm words and phrases that convey your organization's purpose and objectives:

EXAMPLE 5.1

Sample Mission Statement

Organization Function and Customer	Mission Statement
Health-care maintenance organization providing eldercare	Fincon Care ensures that senior citizens receive highest quality, easily accessible services at understandable contract terms.
Software development company selling a range of products for small businesses	Supporting the growth of small businesses by providing a suite of software products that make day-to-day activities more cost efficient and effective, thereby increasing productivity and decreasing overhead costs to the client.
Sales and marketing firm focusing on organic food products	Offering the highest quality in food products to decrease exposure to insecticides and other poisons in our environment.
Financial and insurance product company selling to individuals and organizations looking for a complete product line from one source	afeure provides a family of cost-effective insurance and financial products to a wide range of customers.

1. What does your organization mean to your customers, business partners, the public, management, employees, and executives?
2. What core purpose or theme runs across all of the organization's audiences—customers, business partners, the public, management, employees, and executives?
3. In what ways is the organization *not* of value to your customers, business partners, the public, management, employees, and executives?
4. Why does your organization exist or continue to exist?

When the group has compiled some descriptive and meaningful words and phrases, the "time is write." Compose a draft of the mission statement. If the company already has a statement, be sure you have a copy on hand, either displayed or photocopied for each group member. By writing the mission statement in parts, you can revise each part until you have phrases you believe reflect the scope and direction of your strategic plan. Tool 5.3 identifies the five parts of the mission statement, suggests questions that reveal those parts, and offers examples.

When the group has completed a draft of the mission statement, evaluate it against the criteria set out in worksheet 5.2. Consistency with these criteria will ensure that your mission statement is strong and that it's useful in validating the objectives you specify for your strategic plan (the next creative task we'll tackle).

Creating Mission Objectives

STEP 5

Mission objectives communicate your ultimate purpose or intention for devising the strategic plan. They state the direction you will take and the goals you have. They evolve from your mission statement, and, as you formulate each objective, ask two questions:

1. Does this objective support our mission?
2. By fulfilling this objective, will we meet our mission?

Take a look at example 5.2. There you'll find a sample mission statement and the objectives that flow from it.

Before you begin to write the strategic plan's objectives, you need to understand that these objectives aren't your tactics; nor do they state how you'll respond to the recommendations generated by your data analysis. All of that will come later as you build the specific quantitative action plans or tactical plan for the strategic plan. To help you grasp the difference between objectives and tactics, we suggest you look at example 5.3. The sample is a training company's mission objectives compared with the tactics it proposes to accomplish those objectives.

To develop the objectives for your mission, you'll need copies of your mission statement and the findings, conclusions, and recom-

TOOL 5.3

Parts of the Mission Statement

Mission Statement Part	Defining Probes	Example
Reason the organization exists	◆ What is our organization's purpose? ◆ What is the value we provide to the community? ◆ What is the value we provide to the marketplace? ◆ How would someone outside our organization define or describe us? ◆ What would our customers say is our purpose? ◆ What would a new employee say is our purpose?	To provide cost-effective and appropriate health-care services to low-income families
Organization's customer base	◆ What are the personal and household demographics of our customer base? ◆ Where are our customers located? ◆ Do we have different types of customers (retail, commercial, and so forth)? ◆ How do we reach our customers? ◆ How do our customers reach us (or find us)?	Our customers are often single-parent families who are at or under the poverty level and have no health insurance. We serve our customers by being in locations where public transportation is easily available and we are open 24 hours a day.
Organization's product line or service supplied to our customer	◆ What do we actually provide to customers? ◆ Are our products and services tangible or intangible? ◆ How do we finance our products and services?	We provide basic preventive and urgent health-care and prescription services to

		families. We are funded partially by the government and partially through fundraising efforts in the community.
	◆ What are the benefits and features of our products and services?	
Process used to supply product or service	◆ Who are the suppliers? ◆ What are the steps we use to move the product or service from the supplier to our customer? ◆ Do we have quality controls? If so, what are they?	We use generic drug products from pharmaceutical companies and low-cost hospital products from general health-care suppliers. The suppliers themselves donate much of the general supply.
Marketplace conditions if our organization did not exist	◆ What would happen if we didn't exist? ◆ Would some other organization take our place if we closed? ◆ How long would it take for someone to support our current customer base in our absence?	There is no current supplier in the community that does what we do. Our community would be at greater risk for large-scale breakouts of disease and infection. The families we serve would have a decreased quality of life.

STEP
5

WORKSHEET 5.2

Criteria for Effective Mission Statements

Criterion	Does Your Mission Statement Meet the Criterion?
1. It is concise and to the point.	Yes ☐ No ☐
2. It is fewer than 100 words in length.	Yes ☐ No ☐
3. It defines a scope on which to base strategy decisions.	Yes ☐ No ☐
4. It establishes why we exist.	Yes ☐ No ☐
5. It reflects our competence.	Yes ☐ No ☐
6. It provides focus.	Yes ☐ No ☐
7. It gives us some degree of flexibility.	Yes ☐ No ☐
8. *[if the statement is for a unit or department within an organization]* It is linked to or supports our organization's mission statement.	Yes ☐ No ☐
9. It is realistic and achievable.	Yes ☐ No ☐
10. It can be used for marketing and communication.	Yes ☐ No ☐

mendations from your data analysis. Work with your group to identify at least three but no more than five objectives that reveal the company's purpose and its competitive advantage—why the company is more valuable than others in the same business. Ultimately, these objectives will help you measure how well the company performs.

When the group has developed its mission objectives, use worksheet 5.3 to ensure the objectives will promote value and align with the mission. To use this worksheet, list each draft mission objective

EXAMPLE 5.2

Sample Mission Statement and Corresponding Objectives

Mission Statement: We provide leading-edge training and performance support processes, tools, and products to those organizations that purchase XYZ Company's products and services. We save our customers time and money by training their professionals in our product line, and we customize our product line to meet their specific needs. Our products not only enhance our organization's ability to sell its products and services, but also serve as a revenue chain in themselves.

Objectives:

1. Research new technologies and practices within the industry so we may improve our services and products

2. Evaluate our programs to ensure that they are transferable to our customers' workplaces and that they provide the required business results

3. Benchmark ourselves against others in our industry to ensure that we continually provide products and services that are considered best in class

4. Canvass our clients to ensure that our products and services are considered valuable and priced appropriately

and answer the questions posed in columns 2, 3,and 4. The training company's mission and objectives that we detailed in example 5.2 are included as an illustrative sample in this worksheet.

Creating a Vision Statement

When the writers designated by the group to draft the mission statement and objectives have done their work, and approval for those materials has been received from management, it's time to begin developing the vision statement.

A vision statement asserts where your organization is headed or what its future will be. A vision statement usually has a life of two to four years, and it should support the mission statement and the objectives. The vision statement typically mentions a timeframe and some type of measurement. Here are three examples:

1. Within three years, Morrison Motors will be the number 1 mechanic and auto repair business in the Commonwealth of Virginia.

2. In the next two years, Lulu Imports will increase profits by 150 percent and become known nationally for its unique French housewares.

EXAMPLE 5.3

Sample Mission Objectives and Corresponding Tactics

Mission Objective	Tactic
• Provide knowledge management consulting to our workforce • Become knowledge transfer experts	• Identify knowledge streams critical to our organization's competitiveness • Market our services in knowledge management terms • Demonstrate how we can help our employees gain knowledge and transfer it back to the workplace • Establish knowledge management systems, such as competencies and transfer evaluation techniques
Bring new technologies into our product line in a thoughtful manner	• Devise an e-learning strategy • Investigate technologies that will provide better information to our audience in a more timely manner • Identify our audience's preferences for technology • Measure our audience's readiness for technology
On a regular basis, get feedback from our stakeholders, customers, and business partners concerning their needs for improved organizational performance	• Create a steering committee • Identify ways to perform an ongoing needs assessment of the organization's performance gaps • Identify triggers that change performance needs and devise a method to monitor those triggers
Produce programs that provide measurable results	• Create a measurement system that can report results (or lack of results) • Create program standards • Integrate measurement and standards into our design process

WORKSHEET 5.3

Validating Mission Objectives

Mission Objective	Does It Support the Mission?	Does It Close a Cause-and-Effect Gap?	Does It Support a Recommendation?
Research new technologies and practices within the industry so we improve our services and products	Yes, it helps us stay on the leading edge.	Yes, we need to provide more alternative learning opportunities to our clients.	Yes, our organization's values include continual improvement.
Evaluate our programs to ensure that they are transferable to our customers' workplaces and that they provide the required business results	Yes, we will demonstrate that our programs save our clients time and provide business results.	Yes, by evaluating our programs we will ensure that we provide a value to our customers and provide business results.	Yes, because prospects are asking marketing to provide results back on the job.

STEP
5

155

3. In the next two years, Scott Publications will further develop its business by procuring and publishing a line of cookbooks for time-strapped families, thereby generating more than $1 billion in sales.

Example 5.4 illustrates a framework for developing your vision statement.

One of the issues in writing both mission and vision statements is using generic and broad terms. Often there is an inclination to use buzz phrases such as "leading edge" and "culturally aware." Such wording is rarely descriptive enough to make your meaning clear. Here are two methods for testing the wording of your statements. The first method is to ask people who don't know anything about your business to read or listen to a statement and tell you what type of business you're in or what your organization's future plans are. The second method is to read the mission or vision statement to the strategic planning group and ask if it can discern how much or when or by what means elements of the statements will be accomplished. In other words, can they tell you what "maintain a manageable number of clients" means? Is that 10 or 2,000 clients? Do they know what this community considers to be excellence? Tool 5.4 lists words and phrases to avoid when creating mission and vision statements. These items are overused or have little meaning when they stand alone. If you choose to use any of these words, be sure you define precisely what they mean.

Creating Values Statements

The last task in this step is creating values statements. A values statement should delineate the core values, traits, and qualities the organization expects in its executives, managers, and employees. If the organization is small, these values often are a reflection of the values held by the founder or owner. Values statements define how individuals are expected to behave when representing the organization with customers and business partners and in the community. These values define how decision making is done, how customers

EXAMPLE 5.4

Developing a Vision Statement

Organization Mission	Future Vision	How the Vision Will Be Measured	Goals
Orbach's Department Store specializes in designer and high-end, off-the-rack clothing for professional men and women.	Continue providing professional apparel and expand into business eveningwear for black-tie events and cocktail parties. Also expand into footwear to complement both professional day and evening apparel.	• Timeframe required to achieve the mission • Type of apparel and footwear sold • Increase in revenue from expansion of product line	• Two years • Shoes and eveningwear • $2 billion

New vision statement:

Orbach's Department Store will expand into two new lines of apparel for the professionals they serve. Those lines will be professional evening attire for both men and women, and shoes for both day and evening. This expansion will be completed in two years and will provide an additional $2 billion in revenue for the organization.

TOOL 5.4

Some Vague, Overused, and Potentially Misleading Words and Phrases

Words to Avoid in Mission, Vision, and Values Statements	Phrases to Avoid in Mission, Vision, and Values Statements
Accountability	Best managed
Barriers	Blue-chip clients
Business(es)	Complete package
Community	Culturally aware
Continue	Cutting edge
Culture	Despite controversy
Economy	Double in X years
Excellence	Established leader in
Future	Established leadership position
Global	Full-service
Intellectual	Grow aggressively
Leaders, leadership	Grow conservatively
Minority	Leading edge
Overcome	Major force
Practice	No-compromise
Resistance	The most
Responsibility	
Risk	
World, worldwide	
_____	_____
_____	_____
_____	_____

Also avoid all references to other companies as standards of quality (you can't rely on outside entities to remain in business or maintain an enviable level of performance).

are treated, and what rewards and recognition are given. Tool 5.5 offers a list of values most commonly found in organizations.

Values statements are key to your organization's definition of who it is, and they should support your mission and vision. If, for example, you say you are a family-oriented business, then policies such as

TOOL 5.5

Values Commonly Found in Organizations

Accomplishment	Enthusiasm
Accountability	Ethics
Accuracy	Family orientation
Ambition	Friendliness
Collaboration	Fun
Community orientation	Generosity
Community spirit	Honesty
Compassion	Innovation
Competence	Integrity
Concern for quality	Loyalty
Confidence	Optimism
Courage	Persistence
Creativity	Respectfulness
Credibility	Responsibility
Dedication	Service orientation
Dependability	Spirituality
Determination	Truthfulness
Discipline	Wisdom
Efficiency	

STEP **5**

time off, leaves of absence, funeral and family leave, health care, flex-time, and job sharing should be part of what your organization provides its employees. The values you cite in your values statements and how they are demonstrated reflect the extent to which your organization walks its talk. They should be exhibited by executives, employees, managers, vendors, and suppliers. Give copies of values statements to prospective employees, vendors, suppliers, and others to make clear the behaviors that the organization expects both in the workplace and whenever an individual represents the organization. To illustrate how values statements can be written, we've listed the values statements of three sample companies in example 5.5.

Effective organizations define their values and share their values statements so there is a mutual understanding of what is expected and so everyone's behavior reflects the organization's values.

EXAMPLE 5.5

Sample Value Statements

Type of Organization	Values Statements
Technology company, in business for 3 years	Our values are fiscal responsibility, dedication to getting the job done, innovation, and accountability.
Sales and marketing company specializing in farm equipment, in business for 20 years	We value integrity, customer service, taking pride in our work, presenting accurate information, and sharing ideas.
Amusement park, in business for more than 50 years	We value families, respect, safety, community service, active participation, customer service, and honesty.

◆ ◆ ◆

At this point, you are well beyond the halfway mark in developing your strategic plan, but some of the most important steps are ahead. In Steps 6–8, you'll determine business needs, decide on tactics, and prioritize resources.

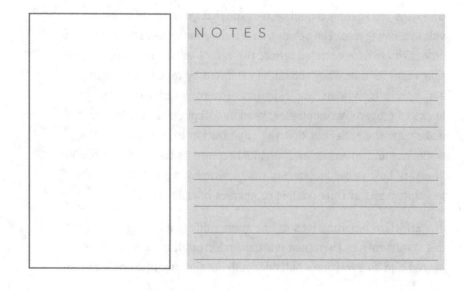

NOTES

Prioritizing Needs and Identifying Risks

OVERVIEW

Setting criteria for prioritizing business needs

Ranking the organization's priorities

Identifying and managing business risks

Creating a decision matrix

STEP 6

The work you've done to scan the business environment, identify business drivers, and articulate or reconfirm the organization's mission, vision, and values has brought you to this point. You should have a clear picture of your organization's tolerance for change and risk and of the unstated rules that affect the organization's politics, decision making, and commitments or sign-offs. You also should have a better understanding of the marketplace in which your organization does business and of the challenges facing it daily. Your mission statement and objectives establish where the organization stands and what it provides to its customers and employees. All of this knowledge is helpful in arranging business needs in their order of descending importance (Step 6) and making decisions about what tactics to pursue for your strategic plan (Step 7).

In any organization, every strategy has resource limitations. There is a finite number of projects and initiatives in which an organization can be involved at any given time, and some are simply more important than others. We all have parameters within which we must work (resources, organizational culture, deadlines, or other

POINTER

constraining factors), and we have to take those parameters into account when we set our priorities so that our expenditures of resources and effort yield the value we advertise.

In Step 6 of *10 Steps to Successful Strategic Planning,* you create criteria for rank-ordering the needs, or priorities, of your business, and this ordering ultimately helps you make decisions about your tactics. These criteria will help you decide (1) which opportunities you should pursue and which gaps you should fill without delay and (2) which you should table for the time being. By revealing what is most important to the organization, the criteria point you toward the tactics that will deliver the most bang for the buck. These criteria will accelerate the development of your tactics in Step 7 and will be valuable tools when you start to execute your strategic plan because they guide your decisions about change.

In this step we'll discuss the following topics:
- establishing criteria to prioritize business needs
- ranking priorities
- identifying and managing risks.

First, let's set the scene with a case example.

Case Example: Prioritizing Needs

This example illustrates how an organization rank-ordered its business needs to help it choose tactics and garner resources.

Setting Priorities for Filling Gaps

Investments Group (IG) is a large, private company that manages various investment funds. Although the organization is rather conservative, it has always funded its various business units very well. In the past three years, IG has acquired several other companies and funds, and is now seen as a global investment management company. With this growth, the organization has found its responsibilities changing and expanding.

While developing its strategy going forward, IG found 10 critical performance gaps that needed attention within the next year. Without discontinuing many of the current programs or greatly enlarging its staff, however, IG probably cannot address all of the gaps within 12 months.

The strategy group discussed the organization's business needs and evaluated them against the mission, vision, and values. This priority setting helped prompt a useful discussion of the trade-offs that management would be willing to accept, with certain provisions, including merging some of the offshore staffing into corporate positions so there would be more flexibility in job assignments. This preparation saved the group time later on as it created its strategic plan and negotiated the resources to implement it.

Establishing Criteria for Setting Priorities

Establishing the priority-setting criteria before you develop the tactics for the strategic plan helps ensure that the tactics will align with the organization's business needs and culture. In later steps you'll use your criteria to validate your tactics and explain the sequence of decisions you made when choosing tactics.

The organizational mapping and business driver identification you completed in Step 2 should have given you an understanding of the values and priorities of the organization, its management, and others closely associated with it. For example, if your organization's marketplace is highly competitive, then initiatives that provide competitive advantage will be most important. However, if your organization has experienced a great deal of turnover and the associated turmoil and costs, retention strategies may have priority.

The mission, vision, and values that have been defined further delineate who the organization is, why it exists, and, most important, what it considers valuable behaviors and actions.

Worksheet 6.1 can help your group identify the organization's principal priorities. Part A lists various priorities that typically compete for resources and effort. From that list, choose five to seven items that you believe would receive the most support and commitment from your customers, stakeholders, business partners, and sponsors. From that assemblage, choose the three to five priorities that bear the greatest importance, and write those in the first column of part B. As you create your action plans in Step 7, use part B to examine how proposed tactics fit the organization's top priorities and choose those you believe are most viable.

Ranking Priorities

You can rank your business needs (and therefore your choice of tactics in Step 7) using the following criteria:

1. *Once-in-a-lifetime opportunity:* This need should be addressed at all costs.
2. *Limitations:* This need is seen as a high priority, but it has limitations (such as budget, resources, risk level, and timeframe).
3. *Scheduling:* This need is important only if it is addressed within a specific timeframe.
4. *Exit:* Results of efforts to address this need are not worth the time and resources they would require.

After you select your principal business needs using worksheet 6.1, use the criteria listed above and described more fully in table 6.1 to rank their importance and feasibility.

Identifying and Managing Risks

Risk is a reality in all organizations, and certainly in strategic planning. Each time you recognize a business need, assign it a priority

WORKSHEET 6.1

Selecting the Organization's Top Priorities

Part A: Choosing among Competing Priorities

Priority	Questions to Ask to Rank Priorities	Notes on Three to Five Top Priorities
Revenue generation	Are product and service sales more than expenses?	
Competitive advantage	Does your company have an advantage over competitors?	
Customer satisfaction	Are customers happy with your product, and will they purchase additional products from you or refer others to you?	
Public perception or reputation	Does your organization have a good standing in the community or industry or with the public?	
Safety	Is your organization considered a safe place to be or to do business with?	
Regulation compliance	Does your company conform to governing regulations?	
Labor availability	Is the appropriate labor, with the right skills and knowledge, available for your organization?	

continued on next page

STEP

6

Worksheet 6.1, continued

Priority	Questions to Ask to Rank Priorities	Notes on Three to Five Top Priorities
Employee satisfaction	Are employees happy that they work in this organization?	
Research and development or creativity and innovation	Are research and development or creativity and innovation valued in your organization?	
Leading edge in the marketplace	Is it important to be seen as a front-runner in the marketplace with your products and services?	
Technological developments	Do you honor technology and feel that technological developments aid in your business?	
Resource availability	Is there the right level of funding? Is the appropriate technology available? Are capital resources available?	
Operational efficiencies	Are the processes and procedures in your organization that are deemed critical or highly necessary documented and available?	
Other:		

Part B: Examining the Fit between Priorities and Tactics

Instructions: In the first column, list the three to five priorities from the list above that you believe are most *important* to your organization. Then complete this section after developing your tactics in Step 7.

Priority	Tactic 1	Tactic 2	Tactic 3	Tactic 4	Tactic 5
	Yes ☐ No ☐	Yes ☐ No ☐	Yes ☐ No ☐	Yes ☐ No ☐	Yes ☐ No ☐
	Yes ☐ No ☐	Yes ☐ No ☐	Yes ☐ No ☐	Yes ☐ No ☐	Yes ☐ No ☐
	Yes ☐ No ☐	Yes ☐ No ☐	Yes ☐ No ☐	Yes ☐ No ☐	Yes ☐ No ☐
	Yes ☐ No ☐	Yes ☐ No ☐	Yes ☐ No ☐	Yes ☐ No ☐	Yes ☐ No ☐
	Yes ☐ No ☐	Yes ☐ No ☐	Yes ☐ No ☐	Yes ☐ No ☐	Yes ☐ No ☐

STEP
6

TABLE 6.1

Criteria for Ranking Priorities

Priority Level	Meaning	Example	Data Source
Once-in-a-lifetime	This is an opportunity for which everything is right and you will never again have the funding, resources, and so forth to respond to it.	Your organization has an opportunity to launch a new line of products. This new line will take advantage of other products you have, but is on the industry's leading edge and offers something to the marketplace that no competitor has. Your findings show evidence that this new product would fly off the shelves and be in high demand for a long time, with little or no redevelopment or advertising.	Such opportunities either emerge during your data search or present themselves unexpectedly as something too good to pass up.
Limitations	Efforts to address this need must fit within certain limitations. Anything outside those limitations is a no-go.	You recognize that no additional staffing resources will be made available to produce the new product line, so production must be completed with existing resources.	◆ Current environment ◆ Research
Scheduling	Addressing this need must be feasible within the master schedule.	You need to develop a succession planning program before the next leadership conference, but when you look at the schedule and the other work to be done, you realize it won't be possible to fit it in.	◆ Current environment ◆ Research ◆ Schedule of events or master schedule
Exit	This business need cannot be filled, or efforts to do so must be retired.	The risk inherent in the product itself, the customer base, and the marketplace are too great to go forward.	◆ Research and data gathering ◆ Organizational mapping, fishbone analysis, and cause-and-effect diagram

STEP 6

Identifying how to manage the risk inherent in your strategy is important, and it will ensure that your mission statement and objectives are fulfilled.

for planning, and begin to consider tactics to address it, you'll encounter some degree of risk posed by the suggested tactics. The degree will vary from need to need. Some risks are potentially more costly than others, and some are easier to manage. The marketplace your organization competes in may be a source of risk, or technological change may be a source. Risk is simply a part of our lives, and it's important to recognize that any overall strategy will have to include risk-mitigation efforts. Identifying how to manage the inherent risks in your strategy is important to ensure that your mission statement and objectives are fulfilled.

Worksheet 6.2 is a risk assessment tool. The statements in the worksheet are based on issues we've encountered in real-life strategic plans. These issues created chaos or delays that almost shelved the strategic planning process. When you've identified which risks your organization faces and how great a level of risk each one poses, note those that are potentially most costly (those rated 3) and then decide how to handle them. You'll need a risk management strategy for each of them. In addition, you should identify any interdependencies or relationships that exist among the statements you rated 3. Usually, the more interdependencies or relationships, the greater the risk to the success of your plan.

Let's consider an example. If you rated the following statements with a 3, it would be important to look at the relationships among them because of the possibility of greater risk. Here are the statements:

◆ The organization must introduce new technology.
◆ Implementing additional efforts will push our capacity, and we will not have the resource allocations needed to handle our current work without compromising quality.
◆ A similar strategy was launched in the past, and it failed.

STEP 6

WORKSHEET 6.2

Assessing Organizational Risks

Instructions: Individually or in a group, review the risk statements in column 1. Rank them on the following scale: 3 = high risk (most likely to happen), 2 = moderate risk (may happen), 1 = low risk (not likely to happen), and 0 = not applicable.

Risk Assessment Statement	Risk Level
Our organization faces a great deal of challenge in the marketplace, and it could cost us our competitive advantage.	3 2 1 0
Implementing additional efforts will push our capacity, and we will not have the resource allocations needed to handle our current work without compromising quality.	3 2 1 0
Our customers definitely will be affected by the outcomes of the strategy, and if something goes wrong, customers will be affected negatively.	3 2 1 0
Employee morale is at stake in the way they view their jobs, the company, and our business; our strategy must address this.	3 2 1 0
There is a lack of definition or purpose for the organization, and expected outcomes are unclear.	3 2 1 0
There is no clear leadership. Either there is no senior manager to whom we report, or it is uncertain where in the organization we belong.	3 2 1 0
Management does not understand the purpose and value of the organization's outcomes.	3 2 1 0
The organization must introduce new technology.	3 2 1 0
The skills and knowledge to support the organization are not present (for example, technology skills are lacking, subject-matter experts are absent).	3 2 1 0
The organization does not have a targeted customer or marketplace.	3 2 1 0
Shareholders or senior managers expect specific outcomes that we must meet, regardless of other needs.	3 2 1 0

STEP 6

Worksheet 6.2, continued

Risk Assessment Statement	Risk Level
The data for the initial analysis for the strategic plan were biased.	3 2 1 0
The strategy has high political visibility.	3 2 1 0
Key systems for the organization may be affected by the strategy.	3 2 1 0
No planning methodology is being followed to develop the tactics.	3 2 1 0
The organization's roles and accountabilities are blurred or undefined.	3 2 1 0
The organization's reputation or market presence depends on the strategy's implementation.	3 2 1 0
Safety could be compromised if we do not address it as a part of our strategy.	3 2 1 0
The organization will not be in compliance with federal regulations unless our strategy successfully addresses compliance.	3 2 1 0
A similar strategy was launched in the past, and it failed.	3 2 1 0

STEP 6

In this example, you have new technology, you don't have the resources to handle the new technology, and a similar strategy already has failed. If you decide to go forward with efforts to address this business need, your stakeholders and managers must be made aware of these related risk factors, and you have to formulate a plan to mitigate the risk.

Worksheet 6.3 is a risk matrix in which you record the risks, suggest actions to mitigate them, and note all other related risks that must be considered. Having this well-rounded view of each risk helps you identify the organizational significance of the risk.

WORKSHEET 6.3

Risk Matrix

Instructions: In column 1, record the areas of highest risk to the organization. Suggest actions to counter those risks in column 2, and note ways in which one risk is related to another risk in column 3. Two illustrative entries are provided.

Area of High Risk	Actions to Control Risk	Related or Interdependent Risks
The strategy has high political visibility.	*We will develop a strong, viable communication plan that is horizontal and vertical.*	*Shareholders or senior managers expect specific outcomes.*
Employee morale is at stake in the way they view their jobs, the company, and our business. Our strategy must address this.	*• We will communicate tactics, outcomes and results, and progress to date throughout the organization.* *• We will gather employee input at key points to ensure that we are making desired progress.*	*• The strategy has high political visibility.* *• Shareholders or senior managers expect specific outcomes.*

Creating a Decision Matrix

If you've encountered any resistance to your strategic planning efforts, be sure you complete all the worksheets presented thus far in Step 6. This thorough examination will ensure the business needs, priorities, and risks are addressed in the tactics you will develop in Step 7.

The decision matrix provided in worksheet 6.4 lists statements that can help you prioritize your business needs. You can use the matrix as a shortcut to setting the priority of various business

WORKSHEET 6.4

Decision Matrix for Business Needs

Instructions: For *each* of the business needs your strategy planning group is considering, complete one copy of this worksheet. For the business need defined below, rate your agreement with the statements in column 1 by circling the appropriate number. Use the scale of 1 to 5, with 1 = strongly disagree, 3 = neutral (neither disagree nor agree), and 5 = strongly agree. Complete one copy of the worksheet for every business need.

Definition of the Business Need: _____

_____

1.	The business need is important to the overall future success of the organization.	1 2 3 4 5
2.	The business need is directly related to (and a critical dependency of) a strategic outcome.	1 2 3 4 5
3.	There is a high degree of confidence that the risk associated with this business need can be managed.	1 2 3 4 5
4.	Outcomes have been identified for this business need.	1 2 3 4 5
5.	The business need is clearly in alignment with the mission statement and what it says the organization is all about.	1 2 3 4 5
6.	There are strong advocates in upper management who believe this need is critical to the organization's future success.	1 2 3 4 5

continued on next page

7.	After reviewing the needs assessment, the strategic team or group believes this business need is a high priority.	1 2 3 4 5
8.	There is a clear cause-and-effect relationship between the business need and the strategic outcomes, objectives, and goals.	1 2 3 4 5
9.	The business need (or fulfillment of the business need) is part of a recommendation.	1 2 3 4 5

Results: If five or more of the statements are rated 4 or 5, this business need should be strongly considered as part of the strategy. If there are some 3s and a mix of 4s and 5s, this business need should be tabled for later discussion. Other scoring outcomes represent a lack of support or justification for the business need at this time.

needs if you have strong commitment to proceed from the strategic planning work group, senior managers, and executives; if the mission, vision, and values have been agreed to; and if there is commitment to the defined outcomes. The business priorities with the highest scores on the matrix are those that are most likely to fit in your organization, make an impact, and be successful.

◆ ◆ ◆

To this point, you've laid a solid foundation for your strategic plan. In the next two steps, you'll take the information, ideas, beliefs, and dreams you've identified and transform them into a realistic plan for the organization's future.

Designing and Validating Tactics

Identifying business
outcomes and measures
for tactics

Validating chosen tactics

Creating the tactical plan

Assigning executive
accountability

An important part of the strategic plan is choosing the tactics. Tactics are activities you select as the appropriate means to gain the desired business results, and they are the meat of the strategic

STEP

7

plan. A tactical plan is the documented, detailed approach for achieving those results.

In most organizations, the strategic plan has a mission and objectives that can exist without change for as long as two or three years, but tactics evolve and mature during that time. When it comes to tactics, the strategic plan should be seen as an evolving and dynamic document that communicates direction, guidelines, and expectations. You should expect to update the tactics on a regular basis, such as every six months.

In this step, we'll discuss methods and tools you'll need to choose and validate tactics. We'll cover the following topics:

- ◆ identifying business outcomes and measures for the tactics
- ◆ validating the finalized tactics against the original scope
- ◆ creating the tactical plan
- ◆ assigning executive accountability.

Case Examples: Choosing Tactics

Here are case examples that describe how two very different companies identified tactics as part of developing their strategic plans.

Linking Tactics to Business Needs and Priorities

Tukamon is a mid-size manufacturing firm. For the first time it has completed a strategy for the entire company. Unfortunately, although the findings from the data gathering have evoked a great deal of passion from those who worked on the strategy, they don't link to the mission, vision, and objectives.

When it reached Step 6 in the strategy development process, the working group spent a lot of time discussing its priorities, the criteria for ranking them, the obstacles and risks associated with the findings, and the process for making good decisions on tactics. The group discussed what needed to change within the organization, the scope and depth of that change, and the processes and structural components required for the change. Then the team talked over the lack of alignment between the findings and the mission, vision, and objectives. Members raised the question, Should the mission, vision, and objectives be revised? After a long and heated debate, the group agreed to focus on findings that would help the organization increase revenue and improve employee and customer satisfaction.

Through this priority-setting analysis, planners and managers established internal operational goals and drew an interactive timetable that provided a bailout strategy for the new tactics that would be devised later in the planning process and a retirement strategy for existing tactics that no longer seemed valuable. They also set up an evaluation matrix to ensure that each chosen tactic would be tightly linked to the priorities that management sought to address.

Developing a Marketing Plan as a Key Tactic

SQ Medical is a medical supply and drug research company with 50,000 employees. The strategic planning work group's data gathering revealed that only a few groups within the organization understood the company's key objectives. The planners also found that customers were generally confused about the services SQ offered and about how they could access auxiliary services for a fee. To address these problems, the strategy group chose to create a marketing plan as one of its key tactics.

SQ felt it needed to be clear about the customers to whom it should market its products, services, and programs, and about what it could promise to deliver so it could avoid overcommitting. In creating the marketing plan, SQ also decided to retire certain programs and to build an ongoing needs analysis process for the programs it offered. These tactics were the foundation of their new strategy.

Identifying Business Outcomes and Measures for the Tactical Plans

An important but often overlooked component of a tactical plan is identifying the expected results for each tactic. In other words, what business outcomes will be realized as a result of effectively implementing the tactic—exactly what should happen if the action is taken? You may find it helpful to choose your expected results from the list of potential outcomes in table 7.1.

Describing and publishing business results and outcomes will provide a mechanism for you to build credibility into the tactics you have chosen. Most senior or mid-level managers are hesitant to be accountable unless they understand how something will help the organization, so you'll have to build your case for gaining their commitment and accountability. Identified business results and outcomes also help you market the plan and its tactics, and help you define the link between personal performance and business performance. It's easier to discuss why workers need to be more inno-

TABLE 7.1

Potential Results or Business Outcomes Realized through Tactics

Business Result	Learning Result	Customer Result	Financial Result
Turnover of inventory is faster	Time to proficiency decreases	Customer satisfaction increases	Revenue increases
Productivity increases	Errors decrease	Customer complaints decrease	Costs decrease
Process improvement occurs	Knowledge increases	Knowledge of customer increases	Market price per share increases
Innovation in products, processes, and programs occurs	Skill increases	Customer retention increases	Net profit before sales increases
Research and development increases	Transfer of new skill and knowledge to the job occurs	Customer product penetration increases	Net profit after taxes increases
Retention of employees increases	Self-confidence about skills and knowledge improves	Retention of key customers (those you really want to stay with the organization) increases	Cost per employee supported decreases

vative when they can see that innovation in products, processes, and programs is part of an overall company responsibility.

Business outcomes often can be measured by

◆ *a count or total of something:* Two hundred new prospects will be identified for product *X.*

◆ *a percentage of an established group:* Thirty percent of the current customer base will be surveyed to ensure their needs are being met with our current products and services.

♦ *a degree of change:* Waste will be decreased by 20 percent by recycling paper products in our offices.

♦ *a dollar amount:* The cost of launching products will decrease through targeting customers and prospects in our new client system. This will reduce our marketing costs by a minimum of $10 million while increasing our product revenue during the week of launch by $25 million.

Worksheet 7.1 is provided as a guide to identifying outcomes and measures for your tactics. An example is provided.

Tactical plans typically fall into one of six categories. Understanding these categories will help you identify metrics for your tactics and will be useful in writing the tactical plan itself. Here are the six categories:

1. *Product and service tactics:* This category comprises the design and delivery of new or enhanced services, products, and programs. Examples include creating a new product as a result of customer input, redesigning a product for a new customer demographic, or localizing a product for a different country. These tactics all involve different ways of delivering the services and products that your organization provides to its clients.

2. *Process tactics:* During your data gathering you may discover that certain processes are not customer friendly or useful. Perhaps they're internal processes, such as an accounting system that doesn't appropriately track budgeting against previous costs. Building a better process for technology delivery, operational improvement, or mechanical support of the organization is considered a process tactic.

3. *Standards and evaluation tactics:* This category involves efforts to control quality. For example, you may need to develop standards to control the quality of output, such as design. Standards and evaluation tactics also can be used for HR purposes, such as a new performance management system or a leadership succession evaluation system. Standards and evaluation tactics are those plans

WORKSHEET 7.1

Identifying Outcomes, Metrics, and Measures

Instructions: In column 1, describe each tactic in your strategic plan. In column 2, describe the expected business result of that tactic. In column 3, describe the expected outcome if the business result is achieved. In columns 4 and 5, define the metric (for example, percentage, count, total, dollars) to be used and the actual measurement terms, respectively.

Tactic	Define the Business Result	Define the Outcome	Define the Metric	Define the Measures
Create a new marketing launch process for new products	As a result, time to market will be quicker because we won't have to develop a new process for marketing each new product that comes out.	A completed process for marketing new products (Product Launch Process) that will decrease time to market by at least 5 percent	Percentage	Decrease time to market by 5 percent

that improve the quality of a product, service, process, or factor that you need to manage to achieve the best result and the fewest errors or defaults.

4. *Organizational and structural tactics:* This category includes tactics that address the need to support a new function or a new area of business, as well as tactics that support the ongoing business of your organization. You might have discovered a need for a marketing and communication leader to handle the development of a monthly newsletter, publish a corporate calendar, compile and distribute reports, and the like. Or perhaps you need to reorganize your human resources to better fit and support the organization's culture and structure. You might need to identify core competencies for your organization so that interviewing, placement, retention, and development can be handled more efficiently and professionally. Perhaps retention is an issue that needs a tactical plan. Any type of organizational or organization structure issues can have tactical plans associated with them.

5. *Marketing and sales tactics:* Ultimately, the way you manage your branding, marketing, and sales is critical to the business. Examples include developing a new sales incentive program (as a new tactical plan), creating a new look, or using a new advertising medium.

6. *Customer tactics:* Your customer base may be changing. You may have an aging demographic with new needs. Or you may find that revised product pricing has drawn new customer types with different needs and demands. Tactics in this category address these issues.

Categorizing your tactics can help you link these tactics back to your mission, vision, and values. By using categories you can group tactics and write one plan that focuses on several interrelated tactics that together focus on a major theme or recommendation. Categories will also help you identify measures, as seen in table 7.2. The first column lists the six categories for tactical measures. As you will see in the second column, where the tactical measures are listed, some are duplicated in several categories. This is important to pay attention to when you are identifying how you want to measure the success of your tactics. If you have several initiatives and can overlap the measurement process by using the measure several ways, you can reduce time. However, be certain that you use additional measures to identify the impact of one tactic to another. For example, if you launch a customer service campaign and lower the price of a product, you might choose to measure both tactics with product price/customer. Most likely, you'd see the price/customer fall, but which tactic was the most beneficial? You would need other measures to isolate the success of each tactic.

Validating the Final Tactics

Measures help validate tactics, but there are other criteria you should consider to validate the tactic before writing and finalizing the tactical plan. For tactics to be valid, three key criteria must be met:

1. The tactic should work to fulfill the organization's mission.
2. The tactic should be related to the goals and objectives that were identified as part of the strategy's outcomes.
3. The tactic should be measurable and its results meaningful to the organization.

A poor tactic would have no relationship to the mission of the organization, would not be related to the goals and objectives, and would be immeasurable. The following example illustrates this point.

Chrissy's Cookies is a national chain. Its mission is "to provide our customers with the finest cookie product while being sensitive to price." One of the tactics it considered was to increase sales training so that sales of higher priced products would increase. When this tactic was evaluated against the first criterion, it was seen to be out of sync with the mission. It wasn't in alignment with what the company perceived as a value (price sensitivity) and consequently was scrapped as a tactic.

Example 7.1 provides a matrix you can use to rate your tactics against the organization's mission, vision, and values statements.

TABLE 7.2

Tactic Categories and Related Measures

Tactic Category	Examples of Related Measures
Process	• Time (start, stop, total) • Cycle time • Equipment cycle time • Safety controls • Days without accident • Audit controls • Inventory controls • Audit results • Pilot or trial results • Performance results • Benchmarking results • Cause-and-effect changes • Changes in work flow • Value activity changes • Time to proficiency • Customer satisfaction
Standards and evaluation	• Time (start, stop, total) • Cycle time • Equipment cycle time • Safety controls • Days without accident • Audit controls • Inventory controls • Audit results • Pilot or trial results • Performance results (as they relate to the process itself) • Benchmarking results • Cause-and-effect changes • Changes in work flow • Value activity changes • Time to proficiency • Customer satisfaction • Costs • Revenue • Cost ratios • Price ratios • Employee satisfaction • Workforce retention
Organizational and structural	• Employee satisfaction • Workforce retention • Salary comparisons with industry • Ability to attract new workers to organization • Placement time

continued on next page

STEP 7

Table 7.2, continued

Tactic Category	Examples of Related Measures
	<ul><li>Time to proficiency</li><li>Organizational results</li><li>Percentage of market share</li></ul>
Customer	<ul><li>Customer satisfaction</li><li>Customer retention</li><li>Cost per customer</li><li>Customer demographics compared with the competition</li><li>Customer perception of competitive advantage</li></ul>
Marketing and sales	<ul><li>Customer satisfaction</li><li>Customer retention</li><li>Cost per customer</li><li>Customer demographics compared with the competition</li><li>Customer perception of competitive advantage</li><li>Percentage of market share</li><li>Price ratios</li></ul>
Product and service	<ul><li>Inventory levels and controls</li><li>Cost per customer</li><li>Customer demographics compared with the competition</li><li>Customer perception of competitive advantage</li><li>Percentage of market share</li><li>Price ratios</li><li>Costs</li><li>Revenue</li><li>Cost ratios</li><li>Price ratios</li><li>Customer satisfaction</li><li>Quality of product/service</li><li>Scrap/reject/rework regarding product/service</li><li>Speed of localizing product and service to new geographic or geopolitical environments</li></ul>

Creating Your Tactical Plans

Now that you have identified whom you are going to serve and
what you are going to offer, the next task is to build your tactics.
Your tactical plan will be an important part of your overall strategy.

EXAMPLE 7.1

Sample Matrix for Recording Alignment of Tactics with Mission, Vision, and Values

	Tactic 1	Tactic 2	Tactic 3	Tactic 4
Mission Statement	3	4	5	3
Mission Objective 1	3	5	5	4
Mission Objective 2	2	4	4	5
Mission Objective 3	5	4	5	5
Vision Statement	2	5	5	4
Values Statement 1	1	5	5	4
Values Statement 2	4	5	5	5
Values Statement 3	1	5	5	4
Values Statement 4	2	5	5	5

By now you've thought about your tactics and how you might measure their success. But how do you get to that success?

One problem that often comes to the fore when finalizing tactics is a confusion of mission objectives and tactics. Table 7.3 explains the differences between the two and provides comparative examples.

After you have identified your tactics, you'll need to develop details for each of them. The content of your tactical plan should include the following six components:

1. *Recommendations*—how the tactics link or support the strategic outcomes
2. *Tactics*—the actions that will be implemented to support the recommendations
3. *Timeline*—a schedule for implementing the tactics

TABLE 7.3

Comparison of Mission Objectives and Tactics

Distinguishing Characteristic	Mission Objective Example	Tactic Example
Mission objectives evolve. Tactics support the evolution.	Develop and implement an overall evaluation strategy	Identify levels of evaluation and the tools to support them that should be a standard for the organization
Mission objectives do not have a clear start and stop. Tactics have a time schedule and completion date.	Improve the selection and performance management of contract instructors	Create instructor standards and implement them by the second quarter
Mission objectives support the mission statement and link to the business. Tactics support the mission objectives.	Create a leading-edge sales curriculum for all levels of sales staff to increase sales and decrease the time-to-close ratio	Develop a sales process leadership program and tie evaluation of it to the time-to-close ratio
Mission objectives define what should be the result. Tactics define how to close the gap.	Ensure that programs are on the leading edge and use front-end technology	Investigate which leading-edge technology adapts to our workplace and will promote learning effectively

4. *Metrics*—the measures that will be used to determine the success of the tactics
5. *Resources*—the resources required to complete the tactics
6. *Assigned responsibility*—the leader of the action.

An example of a tactical plan is presented in example 7.2.

Assigning Executive Accountability

Successful implementation of your tactics is highly dependent on executive accountability for each tactic.

EXAMPLE 7.2

A Tactical Plan

Recommendation: To create a template for launching new products, so as to support the desired outcome of reducing time to market by redesigning our marketing approach.

Measures: Faster time to market, customer satisfaction, decrease in marketing staff development time

Assigned responsibility: Marketing promotion assistant vice president

Tactics to Complete	Timeline	Staff
Develop presentation outline	Q1	KL
Create Webnet strategy	Q2	KL and RB
Build reusable graphics and icons	Q2	RB and TL
Build ongoing communication plan	Q3	KL and RB
Finalize template design	Q3	KL, RB, and TL
Train staff to use template	Q4	TL

Assigned accountability for tactics: J. Fulbright

STEP **7**

The organization's executives should have been involved in the strategic planning process from day 1, and by this point should understand they will be accountable for executing the tactics assigned to them. Executive accountability is critical because your chances for success with your strategic plan will be greatly diminished if top-down accountability is not assigned.

Example 7.3 shows you how to document tactic accountability. For each tactic, note the performance measures by which achievement will be evaluated and the executive who will be responsible for seeing that the performance measures are achieved. When accountability has been assigned and recorded, it's important to share the document with the board of directors and others who are responsible for managing executive performance.

EXAMPLE 7.3

Executive Accountability

Tactic	Performance Measure	Executive Accountable
To increase product penetration with new customers in new geographic locations	• To increase product penetration by 10 percent within 18 months • To identify and expand product within one new geographic location within one year • To identify two new customer groups and increase product penetration for those groups by 5 percent within one year	J. Fulbright, marketing director
To decrease employee costs	• To identify noncritical employee costs that can be reduced within six months • To decrease total employee costs by 4 percent within 18 months	M. Mankolof, senior vice president, HR
To decrease time to market	• To decrease time to market by decreasing product production cycle by 10 days per manufacturing cycle within two years	L. Crepaux, senior vice president, product research and development

◆ ◆ ◆

The next step focuses on methods to prioritize the tactics you've planned and the resources you need to implement them.

Prioritizing Tactics and Resources

Prioritizing needed resources by four kinds of results: customer, business, learning, and financial

Using cost models to prioritize results

If your organization is like most others, resources are scarce—if you go to your sponsor and stakeholders with your strategic plan in hand and ask them to double your budget, it's most likely that you'll be turned down. Whatever additional resources you need, you'll have to spend some time and effort making a strong case to justify those requirements and explain how they relate to the mission objectives and the business.

The tools in this step will help you prepare and present your case and gain the commitment of key people in your organization who will grant you the additional resources. These tools also will help you arrange your tactics in the same order as your organization's needs and objectives. By prioritizing your methods in this manner, you show your business savvy and your willingness to be part of the team—and that raises the planning group's credibility among its stakeholders and business partners.

In this step we'll address the methods you can use to prioritize your resource requests. Specifically, we'll discuss the following topics:

STEP

8

- prioritizing by customer, business, learning, and financial results
- prioritizing using cost models.

Let's begin this step with two case examples.

Case Examples: Prioritizing Resources

Methods of prioritizing resources differ from organization to organization. What works in one may not even be feasible in another. Your understanding of your organization and what it values will help you decide how best to prioritize your resources and present your needs to management stakeholders. Two case examples demonstrate how important it is to understand your organization's structure and the challenges it faces.

Getting a Realistic Grip on Business Needs to Gather Resources

Sportswear Unique is a large sportswear and leisurewear retail company. In completing Step 7 of the strategic planning process, the planners chose three solid tactics directly related to strategic outcomes previously identified and to the organization's mission. Those tactics are

- create an in-depth incentive program for franchises and business partners to sell new products at top prices
- ensure that sale merchandise is sent to outlet locations rather than put on sale at retail stores
- review and change the accounting system to track with new Securities and Exchange Commission (SEC) regulations for retailers.

When Sportswear Unique began to plan the tactics and identify the resources that each tactic would take, planners decided to prioritize the tactics so they could be implemented over the next several years. All parties agreed to the following order of priorities:

1. *The accounting system:* Cost modeling, results, and an assessment of business drivers made it clear that if the or-

ganization did not make the necessary accounting changes, annual reports might have to be restated, SEC fines could be levied, and the company might face even greater penalties.

2. *The move to outlet malls:* The cost to implement this move in year 1 would be relatively low, and making the move would create an additional income stream.

3. *The incentive program:* This tactic was attractive from a sales perspective and management had wanted it to be the top priority, but planners knew that it could be implemented at a later date, whereas the new accounting system could not wait.

POINTER

Whatever additional resources you need, you'll have to spend some time and effort making a strong case to justify those requirements and explain how they relate to the mission objectives and the business.

The strategy design group identified the most critical resources needed to meet the priorities and gained management's approval for these resources. The critical resources were then reassigned and became part of the tactical design implementation team.

STEP 8

Linking Department Tactics and Resource Needs with Corporate-Level Strategy

Electronics Plus is a *Fortune* 100 manufacturer of computer components. It employs more than 10,000 people globally. To stay competitive, the organization needs to pursue an ambitious strategy for the design, development, and delivery of sales and product training.

A subgroup of members from the training department led the prioritization effort by looking at customer, financial, business, and process measures and resources. The subgroup determined that it was really customer and sales knowledge that needed to drive this tactic. Understanding this, the subgroup was able to work with the strategic team and secure the needed resources.

When the organization's strategic planning group completed its tactical plan, it became clear that one year was not long enough to achieve the desired outcomes. Tactics and resources had to be rank-ordered in terms of benefits and value.

The organization emphasizes corporate strategy guiding department and group strategies, so the planners have decided that the best method of prioritizing the department's tactics and resource needs is to link each tactic to a business objective stated in the corporate strategy. Tactics and resources that have weak or no links to the corporate strategy won't be completed in the first year. Acting on this decision, the strategic planning group has chosen four key tactics and have gained strong buy-in from stakeholders and senior managers.

Example 8.1 illustrates a format for linking department and group tactics to corporate strategies. The business drivers, corporate strategic initiative, and business objective are listed in the first three columns, and the department or group tactic chosen to support the corporate initiative is described in column 4.

Prioritizing Needed Resources by Results

To prioritize by results the resources that are needed for your chosen tactics, you must identify the effects a tactic will have on performance, process, behavior, financial, or business indicators. Results can be grouped into four categories: customer, business, learning, and financial. Let's look in greater depth at each category of results.

Customer Results

The customer category involves results that make an impact on service, delivery, or support involving the customer. Here are some

EXAMPLE 8.1

Sample Format for Linking Department and Group Tactics to Corporate Strategy

Business Drivers	Corporate Strategic Initiative	Business Objective	Department/ Group Tactic
• Competition • Revenue generation • Marketplace position	Increase revenues through product launches and other market penetration	Increase sales of new products and reduce time to market and loss of market share	Detailed product information is available through online sales software
• Marketplace position • Customer perception • Competition	Improve marketplace standing by delivering "second-to-none" customer service	Increase competitive advantage by providing 24/7 customer call support	Call center training in telephone troubleshooting escalation, product requests, and new customer setup

examples of tactics that affect the customer (either the organization's customer or the department's customer):

♦ development of a customer service program that promotes call reps' ability to decrease the length of customer calls by training the reps to pinpoint more quickly what information the customer needs

♦ creation of an electronic performance support system that puts product information, typical customer questions, and other key information at call reps' fingertips

♦ development of a customer information system that eliminates the need for customers to reenter data when they change addresses or open additional accounts

♦ initiation of a "know-your-customer campaign" whereby personnel take the time to make contact with their customers and get feedback on their services and programs for future quality enhancements of the product line.

The intent of customer tactics is to align the organization's programs and services more closely to the customer's needs, and to

STEP 8

ensure that customers are satisfied and will continue to see you as the provider of choice. Common customer results are

- improvement in customer satisfaction or end-user perception
- repeat business
- referrals or recommendations
- enhanced public perception of the organization and thereby new customers
- unsolicited positive feedback
- increased relationships
- increased revenue per customer or decreased cost per customer.

Business Results

Business results reflect the influence of tactics on the processes, procedures, research, and development of the organization as a whole. Here are some examples of tactics that may affect the business:

- developing and implementing standards for an accounting system to ensure that errors or noncompliance with regulations are quickly identified and resolved
- streamlining the time needed to prepare marketing materials and product packaging so that time to market is reduced
- identifying methods and processes that encourage employees and customers to offer input and creative ideas to the research and development department so that new products or enhancements to existing products can be developed.

The intent of business tactics is to improve process or work flow or to enhance the creation, innovation, or development of new ideas, new research, or problem resolution. Common business results are

STEP **8**

- improvement in a manufacturing process as a result of a problem-solving course
- decrease in product launch time
- time-to-market decreases
- cycle time decreases
- decrease in material waste
- increase in new product design or realignment
- increase in productivity through streamlining of process time.

Learning Results

Tactics that produce learning results improve the capabilities of the human resources inside the organization. Here are two examples of organizational tactics that may influence learning:

1. training that retools the skills of employees who may experience layoffs and downsizing into the skills needed by a growing department
2. leadership programs that identify high-potential candidates for team leadership positions and then monitor their ability to motivate team members.

The intent of learning tactics is to improve employee morale, alignment with organizational goals and needs, capability, or retention. Common learning results are

- employee suggestions that improve processes or policies
- decreased employee turnover
- employee skill development or enhancement
- increased number of business plans developed by teams with leadership training
- greater number of teams that voluntarily ask to share incentives for work accomplished.

Financial Results

Even seeing the word *financial* makes some professionals nervous. But financial results can be realized from most sound tactics. Tactics that ultimately improve revenue, reduce cost, increase produc-

STEP **8**

tivity, enhance asset utilization, or reduce risk and the resulting cost of risk all produce financial results. Here are several examples:

- development of a streamlined manufacturing process that increases productivity and decreases material waste
- implementation of creativity enhancement programs to produce new goods and services that enhance competitive advantage and increase profits per customer
- launch of a new technology to decrease employee error or increase the time workers can spend on more meaningful tasks
- creation of a branding program that enables customers and prospects to identify more quickly with the product and that creates goodwill in the community
- creation of a sales process package that includes product knowledge development, sales process training, and systems to support the closure of sales
- development of a certification program for production line workers in which training is done on the job and the employees are observed and certified when they meet specific performance levels.

All organizations are concerned with financial objectives. The intent of financial tactics is to align business strategies to ensure the financial health of the organization. Common financial results are

- decreased time to proficiency
- decreased sales cycle time
- decreased time to market
- reduced expenses
- increased sales
- increased revenue generation per employee.

Tool 8.1 can help you identify the results you might expect from your tactics and therefore help you express those results in business terms. For example, if you believe your tactic most likely will decrease a new employee's time to proficiency in product recognition and, ultimately, in sales, then you should describe the tactic as "increasing organizational capacity through rapid product recognition and, ultimately, increasing revenue through sales."

TOOL 8.1

Identifying Tactic Results

Sample tactic description: Design and develop an electronic performance support system that will provide procedures, processes, and troubleshooting information for the organization's call center staff (who resolve customers' problems with products and who process catalog and Web orders)

Part A: Questions to Identify Expected Results (*sample answers are in italics*)

1. What change do you expect for the employee participating in this initiative?
   Increased ability to troubleshoot problems for the customer

2. What impact will this initiative have on the department or group?
   Increased positive perception of the organization

3. What impact will this initiative have on the organization?
   Increased customer satisfaction and decreased time to employee proficiency

4. If there is a process improvement as a result of this initiative, identify what it is and how you will know the results of the process improvement.
   Customer call processes will be in place; call center employee telephone time will decrease and customer satisfaction will remain steady or increase

5. What on-the-job evidence would you look for as a result of this initiative (for example, decreased time to proficiency, increased productivity, increased revenue, decreased costs)?
   Increased productivity, increased customer satisfaction, decreased time to proficiency, decreased time per call

STEP
8

continued on next page

Tool 8.1, continued

6. What overall business impact would you expect from the implementation of this tactic (for example, product sales increase, cycle time decreases, product time to market decreases)?
   Repeat business

7. In business terms, what performance improvement do you expect from this tactic (for example, percentage of error reduction, percentage of sales increase, or number of customer calls completed within a given time per employee)?
   Number of customer calls completed within 15 minutes

8. Can you identify the baseline of the existing level of performance? If so, how (for example, organizational reports, creation of a form for measurement, management evaluation)?
   Yes, through call reports

Part B: Group Measures by Measurement Category

Instructions: In column 2, list the specific measures you have identified for each result category in column 1, and then identify the way in which the tactic will influence that measure.

Result Category	Specific Measure	Tactical Result
Customer	Customer satisfaction	Troubleshooting course will provide call service reps with needed information.
Business	Productivity	Fewer call reps will be needed for call volume.
Learning	Time to proficiency	Call reps will have a shorter period of orientation to the job.
Financial	Resource costs	Decrease in staffing costs is greater than the cost of developing the course.
	Customer retention	Retaining customers is less expensive than recruiting new customers.

Part C: Questions to Analyze Your Identified Results (sample answers are in italics)

1. Is the result understandable to the strategic planning group members, stakeholders, sponsors, and other key business partners within your organization?

   Yes, this result is important to all parties.

2. Is there linkage between the results? If so, how are they linked? (A customer measure, if met, most likely would influence other measures. For example, increased customer satisfaction usually increases sales, referrals and recommendations, and customer relationships.)

   Customers received more accurate and in-depth product information, which increased satisfaction and, therefore, increased sales.

3. Are there any contrary results? (These are results that would make it clear if the tactic did not have an impact—for example, if errors increased instead of decreased, if sales fell, or if time to proficiency increased.)

   If customer dissatisfaction continues, we have a problem.

4. What results are most likely to be seen as valuable by the organization, and why?

   Customer retention and satisfaction, because our customers are a key focus, and the number of competitors vying for our customers is climbing.

STEP

8

When you've identified and categorized the expected results for each of your tactics, it's time to assess the organizational importance of each result. Use worksheet 8.1 to prioritize your tactics and the needed resources using results to identify the more highly valued outcomes. Here are some examples of the resources you may need to implement your tactics:

- human resources, stated in number of full-time equivalents, or FTEs
- systems
- supplier or outsource
- process development
- time
- budget.

You also can use worksheet 8.1 when discussing the following questions about resource allocation:

- Are the results worth the investment of resources?
- Are the results critical to the organization's health?
- Would our stakeholders and management agree that these results are worth the resource investment?
- Should the resources be invested in a more valuable set of results?

Using Cost Models to Prioritize Needed Resources

A cost model can help you prioritize resources by determining the relative cost effectiveness of your tactics. First, you must identify as many costs as possible. Example 8.2 lists various cost categories and potential sources of cost information. Cost information is best compiled using spreadsheet software (such as Excel or any other financial worksheet) so that the calculations can be updated easily as information changes.

This worksheet can be divided into three major categories: (1) the fixed costs (building space, utilities, insurance, taxes, fees and charges), (2) the variable costs (professional fees, inventory, ship-

WORKSHEET 8.1

Prioritizing Tactics and Resources by Expected Results

Instructions: List each of your tactics in column 1 and, in column 2, identify the resources needed to support each tactic. In column 3, list the results you expect to realize when each tactic is implemented. Be realistic! Finally, in column 4, rank the importance of each tactic's results (all of the results as a package) to the organization. Rank them on a five-point scale (5 = very important, 3 = somewhat important, and 1 = very unimportant). Two examples are offered here as illustration.

Tactic	Resources Required for Tactic	Results Expected	Importance of Results to Organization
Install a new accounting system to track regulatory errors	• 5 FTEs to study current system • 3 FTEs to program and test new system interface with current system • 2 FTEs to conduct pilot test and report results • 1 FTE to train staff to use system	• Decrease in regulatory issues • Decrease in penalties • Decrease in accounting errors • Increase in compliance with SEC guidelines for public retail companies	5 ☒ 4 ☐ 3 ☐ 2 ☐ 1 ☐
Development of employee health courseware	• 2 FTEs to design courseware • 2 full-time subject-matter experts • External wellness consultant ($15,000)	• Decreased absenteeism • Increased energy • Decreased turnover • Improved employee morale	5 ☐ 4 ☐ 3 ☒ 2 ☐ 1 ☐

continued on next page

STEP
8

Worksheet 8.1, continued

Tactic	Resources Required for Tactic	Results Expected	Importance of Results to Organization
			5 ☐ 4 ☐ 3 ☐ 2 ☐ 1 ☐
			5 ☐ 4 ☐ 3 ☐ 2 ☐ 1 ☐
			5 ☐ 4 ☐ 3 ☐ 2 ☐ 1 ☐
			5 ☐ 4 ☐ 3 ☐ 2 ☐ 1 ☐
			5 ☐ 4 ☐ 3 ☐ 2 ☐ 1 ☐

EXAMPLE 8.2

Sample Worksheet for Identifying Tactic Costs and Benefits by Month

Cost/Benefit Categories	Month 1	Month 2	Month 3	Month 4	Month 5	Month 6	Month 7	Month 8
Fixed-cost categories:								
Facilities cost (build, lease, rent month to month)	($20,000)	($20,000)	($20,000)	($20,000)	($20,000)	($20,000)	($20,000)	($20,000)
Utilities	($4,000)	($4,000)	($4,000)	($4,000)	($4,000)	($4,000)	($4,000)	($4,000)
Insurance	($1,500)	($1,500)	($1,500)	($1,500)	($1,500)	($1,500)	($1,500)	($1,500)
Taxes, fees, and charges	($3,000)			($3,000)			($3,000)	
Licenses	($12,000)							
Subscriptions	($600)							
Membership dues		($1,000)				($600)		
Equipment or systems		($100,000)						
Variable-cost categories:								
Payroll	($20,000)	($30,000)	($32,000)	($29,000)	($50,000)	($51,000)	($49,000)	($50,000)
Payroll taxes	($2,000)	($3,000)	($3,200)	($2,900)	($5,000)	($5,100)	($4,900)	($5,000)
Training	($1,500)			($35,000)	($2,000)	($2,000)	($2,000)	($140)
Loan costs and fees	($3,500)			($200)	($4,700)	($2,100)		

continued on next page

STEP
8

Example 8.2, continued

Cost/Benefit Categories	Month 1	Month 2	Month 3	Month 4	Month 5	Month 6	Month 7	Month 8
Bank service charges and fees	($35)	($701)	($283)	($128)	($789)	($987)	($552)	($123)
Travel costs	($4,500)		($2,700)	($11,000)	($3,500)	($38,000)	($20,000)	($27,000)
Professional fees or consultants, external resources	($2,500)			($40,000)	($40,000)			($12,000)
Inventory costs				($250,000)	($27,000)		($75,000)	($120,000)
Shipping costs							($3,500)	($2,750)
Advertising	($500)					($4,000)	($8,000)	($22,000)
Accounting		($2,400)		($320)	($4,000)		($810)	($8,800)
Purchasing		($400)	($75)		($157)	($821)		($232)
Graphics, printing								($982)
Entertainment, food, refreshments				($200)	($352)			
Incentives or giveaways					($500)	($1,000)	($1,750)	($1,000)
System development (Web-site inventory tracking system)				($400)	($750)	($329)		
Work disruption costs (training, moving, and the like)				($2,000)			($37,000)	

One-time cost categories:

	Month 1	Month 2	Month 3	Month 4	Month 5	Month 6	Month 7	Month 8
Hardware acquisition	($25,000)							

Software acquisition				
Relocation of accounting staff	($75,000)	($400,000)	$80,000	
				$200,000

Benefit categories:

Human resources benefits (decreases in costs; increased productivity; increased retention; decreased time to proficiency; increased morale, knowledge, and/or skill enhancement; decreased labor costs; shortened learning curve, and so forth)			
Customer benefits (decreased customer turnover, increased product-to-customer ratio, decreased customer/account cost, increased customer knowledge, increased customer satisfaction, decreased customer errors, and so forth)	$300,000		
Process benefits (increased productivity, elimination of productivity or delivery bottlenecks, improved quality, reduced scrap or material waste, decreased redundancy and lower costs produced by use of integrated systems, and so forth)			

continued on next page

Example 8.2, continued

Cost/Benefit Categories	Month 1	Month 2	Month 3	Month 4	Month 5	Month 6	Month 7	Month 8
Learning benefits (increased productivity, enhanced morale, increased opportunities for optimizing internal staffing, increased skill levels, deeper company culture, and the like)				$200,000				
Financial benefits (lower costs, increased revenue, improved financial ratios, increased attractiveness to shareholders, increased reinvestment opportunity, and so forth)								$500,000

ping, commissions, advertising, accounting, purchasing), and (3) the benefits (human, customers, processes, business and financial). There also may be one-time special costs, such as hardware acquisition or software package acquisition, that should be identified.

When you've gathered the cost information, you'll need to build a budget for your chosen tactics. Example 8.2 illustrates such a budget, and it forecasts when a tactic will result in some sort of savings (the benefits to be realized for the costs invested). For example, note the payroll line in example 8.2. In the first few months, payroll is under $35,000. As the product comes closer to its launch, more resources and more overtime are necessary to meet deadlines (months 5–8). Another example is in inventory costs. No expenses occur until prelaunch in month 4, and then restocking occurs in months 7 and 8. You also may want to break out the costs by tactic or provide costs for each tactic with a running total for the overall strategic plan so that the investment in the tactic is clear. When you have completed this work, you'll have an estimate of the start-up costs for each tactic. It's very important to identify and estimate the costs of each tactic for at least six to 12 months. For some tactics you might even have a two- or three-year model. When you've plotted the costs and discovered if any costs are optional, you have a sound start-up budget.

You may need to consult specific cost-model worksheets to identify such costs as a person-month calculation for software development. (A model called COCOMO is sometimes used for this purpose. For additional information and examples of cost models, a good Website to visit is www.softstarssystems.com.) Or perhaps a group of resources must be moved from one location to another for a specific period of time—for example, to launch a new store or work on a specific product. In that case, you may need to use a cost-of-living calculator to identify wage adjustments, cost-of-living comparisons, moving costs calculations, and even a salary calculator. If you start doing business in a new country and need to project the costs in a different currency, then you'll need a universal currency converter. There are also specific cost models for particular industry needs, such as purchasing, advertising and marketing, and human resource development. An Internet search can be very helpful in identifying online models to use for your initial estimates.

STEP

8

Another cost that is sometimes difficult to quantify is human resource allocation. Example 8.3 illustrates a worksheet to help you identify and justify the human resources needed to implement your tactics and, ultimately, your strategic plan. This worksheet describes the additional specialized resources you need to implement

EXAMPLE 8.3

Sample Worksheet for Identifying the Human Resources Needed to Implement Tasks (Additional Workforce Needs)

Resources Needed/ FTEs	Need	Benefits of Adding These Resources	Have/Can Borrow	Need to Find
8.2 FTEs	Programmers with retail experience	Deadline to implement new system is short and critical for regulation purposes; additional resources will help us meet the deadline	5.8 FTEs	2.4 FTEs
3 FTEs	Retail process analysts	Analysts understand retail accounting and franchises, as well as retail store processes	2.5 FTEs	0.5 FTE
0.5 FTE	Marketing and communication manager	The right manager will be able to communicate changes to employees and customers and build a communication strategy that will "sell the changes"	0 FTE	0.5 FTE
2 FTEs	Trainers for system and end-use customer training	Not applicable	2 FTEs	0 FTE

your tactics, asks you to explain how the additional resources will contribute to the success of the plan, and gives space to note the number or amount of resources you have on hand or can borrow and the number or amount you have to find.

The example indicates if an increase of full-time equivalents will be needed, and where you will need those resources—and that provides for better resource planning and prioritization. You should create and complete a similar worksheet for each tactic.

Presenting to your stakeholders and, perhaps, executives the information contained in worksheets you model after the worksheets illustrated in examples 8.2 and 8.3 should trigger spirited discussions about the proposed investment and the expected results. If costs are of concern or if the tactic is considered a high-ticket item, you may want to combine the results-based prioritization with the cost-based prioritization to create a cost analysis (see tool 8.2 for a description of the seven steps needed to complete a cost analysis).

Another way to help executives and others understand the value of a tactic is to calculate the return-on-investment (ROI)—the benefits that the tactic will pay. Using the information you already have gathered, here's a basic three-step process that can illustrate the tactic's pay-off to the organization:

1. *Calculate the value of the tactic's benefits.* If a tactic will provide specific benefits, identify the monetary value those benefits will yield. (You can use the information you gathered for your cost-benefit analysis, as illustrated in example 8.2.)
2. *Determine the total cost of the tactic.* Using the same information, identify the total costs (fixed, variable, and one-time), and calculate the monetary value.
3. Compute the tactic's ROI.

STEP 8

Here's an example of an ROI calculation:

$$ROI = \frac{\text{Total benefits} - \text{Operating costs}}{\text{Investment costs}} \times 100$$

TOOL 8.2

Cost Analysis Process

Description of Process Step	Desired Results
1—Identify the business and performance need that you are trying to meet. Identify what the business result of the tactic will be (see tool 8.1 and worksheet 8.1).	Identification of the factors, performance indicators, and changes you wish to effect Identification of the benefit the tactic will provide
2—Consider alternatives. Present information on different alternatives or methods. Would it be more practical to do it one way or another?	Comparison of the alternatives or different tactics you are considering
3—Use budgeted, estimated, or actual costs known to date to identify tactic costs (see examples 8.2 and 8.3).	Identification of all probable costs
4—Identify the benefits and potential value of each benefit to the organization (for example, increasing sales by 3 percent would generate $100,500 in revenue for the organization).	For a cost-benefit analysis, a listing of all the dollar costs and all the benefits
5—Finalize the costs and values. Review the costs and benefits with the stakeholders and gain agreement.	Final list of the costs or cost forecasts to date
6—Compare the costs against the benefits.	Determination if any potential costs (or cost savings) or benefits have been missed (for example, the plan should specify that a cost for equipment does not need to be incurred because the equipment was funded by a previous project in the past year)
7—Create a summary of the data gathered in this process, and gain agreement on the tactic.	Final list of costs and benefits that can be reviewed during the implementation of the tactic to ensure that your group is on track

Source: Adapted from S. Barksdale and & T. Lund, "Justifying the Cost of an EPSS," *Technical Training* 8(7): 16–20.

Using calculations based on your cost-benefit worksheet, add the monetary value of the benefits and subtract the tactic's fixed and variable costs. You would then divide the total by the fixed costs and multiply the quotient by 100. This number represents a percentage of ROI. Anything over 100 percent is a "value-add" to the organization. Anything less than 100 percent means the tactic won't add monetary value to the organization (although there may be nonmonetary reasons to pursue the tactic, such as regulatory requirements, company philosophy, or other value that can't be quantified in financial terms).

The worksheets that prioritize costs and results can be powerful tools for selling your tactics to stakeholders, executives, managers, and others inside and outside of your organization. However, as Electronics Plus realized in the second case example, you also can prioritize resources and gain commitment by aligning your tactics with the business objectives, strategic initiatives, and business drivers.

Providing this information to your stakeholders and executive management indicates the amount of thought and analysis that went into identifying the expenses. This is a positive indicator that an equal amount of expense monitoring and managing will go into implementing the tactics. This type of information is extremely useful to executives because it equips them to make better and more informed decisions.

STEP **8**

◆ ◆ ◆

When you've established your tactics and prioritized the resources you need, you're ready to start documenting and communicating your strategy. In letting stakeholders know about the plan, you may want to give them the tools you used in this step to demonstrate your thought process and to link your plans explicitly to the business.

N O T E S

STEP
8

Documenting and Communicating the Plan

Making a record of your strategic plan

Creating a plan for communicating the strategy

Tailoring the message to various audiences: stakeholders and advocates

One major reason that strategic plans fail is they never are communicated to stakeholders. Documenting and communicating the strategy shouldn't be a stumbling block in the overall process, but setting the plan down in some written form and publicizing it may seem to require more effort than does executing the plan. This step focuses on making these activities easier so that the real work can get done. We'll give you information and tools for documenting and communicating your strategy in a way that's useful, continuous, and practical.

Case Examples: Documenting and Communicating

How you record and publicize your strategy depends on your organization, its culture, and its communication norms. The following two case examples illustrate this.

POINTER

Strategic plans fail if they are not communicated to stakeholders.

Balancing Competing Concerns

As part of its strategic plan, the HR division of Dalmar was to revise the current succession planning program. New measures were put in place to determine the program's success.

How the employees were made aware of the program was crucial because the company now required them to apply for program participation, and their acceptance would be measured using new criteria. Dalmer, however, didn't want to lose employees who might grow disgruntled if they weren't eligible for the new program.

These competing concerns demanded a sensitive communication package that explained the changes, why the changes were being made, and how employees who were eligible for the old program could be involved in the new succession planning program.

Breaking the News Creatively

Wagner's is a network of retail stores. Through research and brainstorming, the strategic planning team identified three key tactics—one for each of the strategic outcomes. The first outcome was to increase store safety through education and continuing communication of safety tips. The second was to increase the level of customer service for new customers while maintaining the high level of service that long-term customers expect. The third outcome was to decrease losses through product returns.

Explaining the programs related to each of those outcomes in a way that would minimize employee resistance was vital. Planners feared that most employees would think, "Same old, same old," so they created an employee activity for each outcome. For example, for the first outcome they hired actors to stage safety incidents and then hand the employees flyers that highlighted the new safety program and told them whom to contact for more information.

Each program and activity associated with an outcome was innovative and creative. Employees had fun with the activities and felt the organization was breaking away from old processes. They were excited about their participation in the new programs.

Documenting the Strategic Plan

The plan is finished. You've developed a set of tactics, assessed risk, and identified and prioritized needed resources. Now you must record the strategic plan and create a mechanism to communicate it to the rest of the world.

Documenting the strategic plan will give you a valuable marketing tool and an audit trail for identifying what you plan to do and how you will track your progress. Much of the work that was completed in previous steps of this process can be transferred to the strategic plan document.

Tool 9.1 is an outline to help you record all the aspects and supporting information for your strategic plan. Each section of the outline is described and its contents are enumerated. Likely sources for the information that you'll record in each section are listed in the third column.

Using tool 9.1, a small subgroup of the people who have worked on the strategic plan can prepare the first draft of the strategy record. The larger group then can review and comment. When a second draft that incorporates the larger group's input is completed, distribute that draft to senior managers and, if appropriate, to your organization's board.

STEP 9

Several important pieces of supporting information should be added as appendixes to the plan. These include
- specific action plans to carry out the various strategic tactics
- highlights of the data analysis, including the SWOT analysis
- a summary of issues that were discussed during the planning
- a list of goals specified by senior management and directors
- high-level budget goals that will become the budget plan as the organization goes forward

TOOL 9.1

A Strategic Plan Outline

Section	Content of the Section	Potential Sources for Content
Strategy overview: Much like an executive summary for a much larger report, the overview focuses on the expected end results of the strategic plan and on the contents of the overall strategy document.	• Definition of the mission and objectives • Discussion of the research done to identify the mission and objectives • Brief discussion of the conclusions and recommendations and how they relate to the objectives • Overview of the contents of the strategy document	• Tools from Step 5 for the mission statement and objectives • The findings, conclusions, and recommendations report created at the end of Step 4 for the research findings
Strategy charter: Outlines the mission and objectives and the supporting tactics; identifies the strategy's importance to the business; and describes the benefits of the mission, objectives, and tactics.	• Mission statement • List of mission objectives • List of tactics • Definition of the relationships among the mission, objectives, and tactics • Validation of the benefits to be realized by implementing the tactics, meeting the objectives, and fulfilling the mission	• Tools from Step 5 for the mission statement and objectives • An overview of the tactical plan created in Step 7
Description of current environment: Briefly outlines where the organization, unit, or department is today, the resources deployed, the type of work performed, and any problems or missed	• Identification of current roles and accountabilities • Brief overview of the services and products provided by the organization, department, or unit	Organizational mapping from Step 2

opportunities; may discuss why the strategic plan was developed.	• Description of missed opportunities and the organizational costs of not pursuing them	
Findings from research and data gathering: Summarizes the research completed before or during strategy development; records the conclusions and recommendations.	• Detailed discussion of the research and data-gathering methods, their objectives, and the key findings from each method • Compiled conclusions and recommendations of the research • Summary description of how the findings were used to build the strategy	• Findings, conclusions, and recommendations report from Step 4 • Brief discussion of how the findings and cause-and-effect analyses were used to create the strategy
Tactical plan: Details the actions the organization expects to take; may also identify additional work that must be done and who will be responsible for completing the work.	• Description of the tactics • Explanation of the plan for implementing each tactic, including identifying person responsible for any follow-up to ensure the tactic is implemented • Description of the links between the business needs identified in the data-gathering and the tactics chosen to address them	• Tools from Step 7
Team roles and accountabilities: Briefly describes each projected team role and identifies the outputs for which the person occupying that role is accountable.	• Identification of the roles for the employees who will implement the strategic plan • Description of the duties of and benefits for those roles	• Tools from Step 8

continued on next page

STEP

9

Tool 9.1, continued

Section	Content of the Section	Potential Sources for Content
	• Description of how the roles link to the tactics	• Tools from Steps 6 and 7
Expected results: Identifies potential measures for the tactics and the success of the strategy.	• Listing of resource criteria • Explanation of team metrics • Definition of strategy success metrics	
Resource requirements: Details the resources needed and the potential costs and sources for each of the tactics.	• Description of staffing requirements • List of costs for each tactic, such as technology acquisition, equipment purchase, and other expenses • List of capital expenditures	• Tools from Step 8
Recommended next steps and follow-up actions: Describes what must happen next to implement the strategy; outlines how the strategy will be maintained and updated as issues arise or time passes.	• List of the next steps the organization, department, or unit will take to implement the strategy • Maintenance plan	• Tools from Steps 9 and 10

STEP
9

- the evaluation plan or the measures to be used to determine if the plan is working effectively
- a glossary to explain acronyms, industry-specific words and phrases, or other terms that may be specific to your organization
- a sign-off page listing the individuals who have committed to the plan itself, usually including key members of the planning committee, senior managers, board members, and those who ultimately will be held accountable for the goals, objectives, and outcomes of the strategic plan.

Communicating Your Strategic Plan

POINTER

Communication materials should be separate from the plan itself to ensure that sensitive competitive information is not shared with people who shouldn't have it.

When all parts of the record have been combined to document the strategic plan, the record can be used to develop materials for communicating the plan to stakeholders. Keep the plan documents separate from your communication materials to ensure that sensitive competitive information is not shared with people who shouldn't have it. This will enable you to position your communication as appropriate for various audience needs.

Effective communication directly motivates the actions that must be taken to ensure results and, ultimately, to make your strategy successful. A well-reasoned communication plan and the proper tools enable an organization to

- identify and overcome resistance to the strategy itself and to the actions required to execute it
- strengthen relationships among employees and promote the perception that they are participating in the plan rather than having it imposed on them

STEP 9

- focus on the results and outcomes rather than simply on the process
- gain access to needed resources or information more easily because of enhanced credibility
- create a cohesive environment by unifying resources to achieve commonly desired outcomes
- maintain a focus on useful information rather than being sidetracked by secondary issues
- gain commitment to the strategic and tactical plans.

The reasons why communication planning is important can vary. Some of the more common reasons are to

- explain why the strategic plan is being introduced *now*
- describe what's in it for each party and how each will benefit
- promote adequate planning by describing the required resources and setting a time when they will be needed
- answer employee questions about how their jobs will be affected by the strategy
- provide a public record of intentions and to discourage rumors
- define relationships among business partners
- document commitments made to customers and customer satisfaction.

Many factors can affect the type of communication media you choose, how you develop the communication plan, its degree of complexity, and which supporting tools it uses. We've described some of these factors in table 9.1.

A Six-Step Communication Planning Process

We recommend that you use the following six-step process to prepare a sound communication plan:

1. *Formulate the key messages.* Define the statements that convey the most crucial information about the strategy (such as, why increasing competitive advantage is being done at this time). An example of a key message is, "With

TABLE 9.1

Factors That Affect How the Strategy Is Communicated

Factor	Impact
Time	A short timeframe often dictates the medium for communications, such as email, voice mail, or brief meetings.
Size or complexity	The size or complexity of the strategic plan directs the type of communication that will ensure success. Communicating a strategy with 15 tactics is very different from explaining a plan with five tactics.
Culture	The culture of an organization must be considered in planning the communications. Some cultures are consensus driven and gather everyone's opinions. Other cultures value individual performance and accountability.
Project visibility	• Strategic projects often are highly visible and may inspire rumor and conjecture. A well-reasoned communication plan nurtures a cohesive and trust-based environment. • Understanding the organization, its products and services, and how they will be affected is important to the strategic plan.

this strategy, we will increase our competitive advantage by developing systems that help our employees better understand our customers and their product and service relationships. We will work to understand how we can improve the quality and delivery of our products and services to increase customer satisfaction and market share, and leverage our position among our competitors."

2. *Identify your audiences and select the messages they should receive.* Decide whom you're addressing—managers, employees, customers, the public at large. Then decide if and how the message needs to be tailored for each audience. Whereas investors might be interested in how your organization will increase revenue by $10 million in three

years, your customers will be more interested in the new products you're introducing and how those products will benefit them.

3. *Identify communication points and establish a communication timetable.* Communication points—milestones or significant events that occur while the strategic plan is being implemented—include those times when the tactics are kicked off, when needed resources have been identified, when the budget has been finalized, and when the strategy is implemented. A timetable for the events should be part of the strategic plan. Your timetable will be highly dependent on your organization and the elements of your strategy.

4. *Gather resources to support communication and information distribution.* Identify and secure the resources you'll need for the communication plan, including Internet developers, telecommunication specialists, performance specialists, and others who'll help deliver the message or supply needed resources such as funding.

5. *Develop and pilot test your materials and vehicles.* Create and test the communication vehicles. Because the tools you can use as communication vehicles vary widely, it's wise to pilot test the ones you've selected with a small audience. This will help you discover if the message you want to deliver is the one being received, and it will point out any missing information that might negatively affect the success of the organization's strategy.

6. *Distribute communication materials.* Disseminate your message to your audience through whatever channels you've chosen.

The flowchart in figure 9.1 illustrates this six-step process. It is considered a best-practice communication plan because several leading companies have used it successfully to communicate their strategic plans. This visual will help you frame a communication strategy that will explain your vision.

Your documented strategic plan is an invaluable communication tool. You can use it in its entirety to describe your mission and tactics, or you can use parts of it to give specific information to a targeted group. Tool 9.2 describes each component of a master communication document. The strategic plan itself is the source for

TOOL 9.2

Components of a Communication Document

Component	Definition
Executive summary	This is a brief version of the strategic plan, written for external audiences—the public, investors, prospective customers, business partners, and others who want to know where the company is going in the next few years, and why. This is a key piece of any communication plan.
Organizational background information	This is the historical viewpoint. It discusses where the organization has been and where it is at present. It may include key products, customers, and business partners as well as an organization chart reflecting the current structure.
Mission, vision, values	Taken straight from the strategic plan, these statements reflect "the personality" of the organization and the reason it exists. This is an important component for both internal and external communication pieces.
Outcomes, goals, objectives	This is primarily an internal component, although it might be shared externally and so cannot contain too much sensitive information.
Tactics, resources	This component is a high-level summary of the tactics that have been put in place and the resources needed to achieve the expected outcomes.
Commitment and authorization	This is a list of the people who have committed to and authorized this plan. It's an important part of the communication package not only for employees but also for investors and business partners, so that all may understand the level of commitment across the organization.

STEP 9

FIGURE 9.1

Communication Planning Flowchart

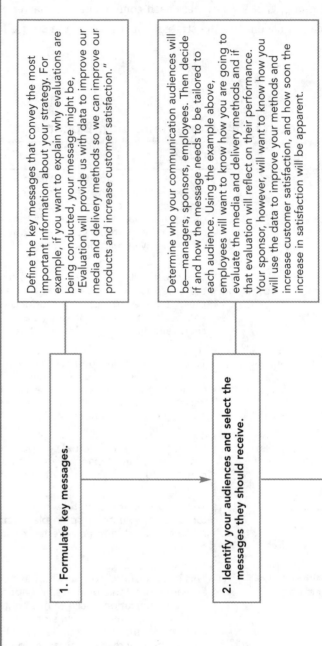

1. Formulate key messages.

Define the key messages that convey the most important information about your strategy. For example, if you want to explain why evaluations are being conducted, your message might be, "Evaluation will provide us with data to improve our media and delivery methods so we can improve our products and increase customer satisfaction."

2. Identify your audiences and select the messages they should receive.

Determine who your communication audiences will be—managers, sponsors, employees. Then decide if and how the message needs to be tailored to each audience. Using the example above, employees will want to know how you are going to evaluate the media and delivery methods and if that evaluation will reflect on their performance. Your sponsor, however, will want to know how you will use the data to improve your methods and increase customer satisfaction, and how soon the increase in satisfaction will be apparent.

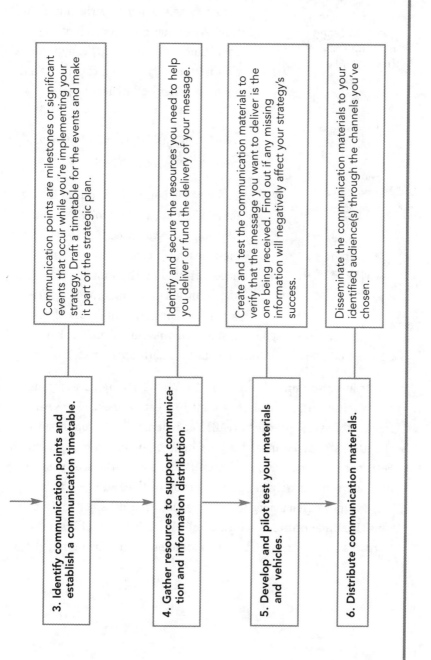

3. Identify communication points and establish a communication timetable.

Communication points are milestones or significant events that occur while you're implementing your strategy. Draft a timetable for the events and make it part of the strategic plan.

4. Gather resources to support communication and information distribution.

Identify and secure the resources you need to help you deliver or fund the delivery of your message.

5. Develop and pilot test your materials and vehicles.

Create and test the communication materials to verify that the message you want to deliver is the one being received. Find out if any missing information will negatively affect your strategy's success.

6. Distribute communication materials.

Disseminate the communication materials to your identified audience(s) through the channels you've chosen.

STEP
9

POINTER

You should include the following audiences when communicating messages about your strategic plan:
- sponsors
- supporting resources
- stakeholders
- business partners
- investors
- employees
- vendors
- the community at large
- customers (if appropriate).

these sections. When the components are gathered, the document can then be edited to delete any sensitive information. When you have completed the communication document, copy information from it to prepare different materials for a variety of audiences.

Tailoring Your Message to Specific Audiences

Different audiences need to hear different messages. You can use tool 9.2 in conjunction with worksheet 9.1 to select the messages you'll communicate to audiences affected by the strategic plan. You should include the following audiences when communicating messages about your strategic plan: sponsors, supporting resources, stakeholders, business partners, investors, and customers (if appropriate).

If in-person presentations or live Web chats are part of your communication plan, you may want to create a sheet of answers to frequently asked questions (FAQs). It's an excellent prop or aid for the presenter and a great handout or Web posting to get answers to FAQs out to users, customers, stakeholders, and others. If your organization has a Website, post a version of the FAQ sheet that visitors can print (remember to use a version that does *not* contain sensitive organizational information). Worksheet 9.2 offers questions that often are asked when a strategic plan is being rolled out.

STEP 9

WORKSHEET 9.1

Directing Messages to Specific Audiences

Instructions: Imagine that *you* are one of those people to whom you want to communicate a message—a member of a specific audience. Ask yourself the questions in column 1 to discern the key messages about the strategic plan that you want to communicate to a specific audience. In column 2, describe the audience(s) that should receive each message.

Message Question	Target Audience
1. What role will I need to play in the execution of the strategy? How much time will I need to commit to this project?	
2. How does the execution of the strategy affect me, or my staff, or others?	
3. How does this strategy fit in our culture?	
4. What kind of changes can I expect?	
5. What is the timetable for the execution of the strategy?	
6. Who are the sponsors?	
7. What are the benefits of the execution of the strategy for our organization, for my staff, and for me?	
8. What are the expected results and outcomes of the executed strategy?	
9. How will this be different or similar to what the training group currently performs in our environment?	
10. How will the strategy and its tactics be kept up to date and linked to our business?	
11. Whom do I contact if I have further questions about the strategy or its execution?	
12. How can I keep updated on the status of the execution of the strategy and its results?	

STEP **9**

WORKSHEET 9.2

Frequently Asked Questions

Instructions: Answer the questions presented in column 1. Add other questions you believe might be generated by your strategic plan.

Frequently Asked Questions	Answer
What changes can we expect, and when?	
What is the budget for the changes?	
How do the tactics link to the organization's strategy and performance needs?	
How will the execution of this strategy improve our business?	
What are the next steps?	
Whom do I contact with questions?	
What supporting material is available (online or on paper)?	
How long will the execution of the strategy take? What kind of job interruption might be part of the execution?	
What are the benefits of executing the strategy versus keeping the status quo?	

◆ ◆ ◆

When the plan has been documented and explained to all appropriate audiences, its execution begins. To ensure the strategy stays up-to-date and effective, the final step in this 10-step process addresses ways to develop a strategy maintenance plan.

Maintaining the Plan

OVERVIEW

Identifying common maintenance triggers

Deciding between updating and rewriting

Setting a plan review schedule

Although it's one of the most important steps in the process, this last step is seldom completed. You've worked hard to develop a strategic plan, and you've documented and publicized it successfully. Now your task is *not* to put it on the shelf and consider the process complete. It's not unusual for planners to accomplish steps 1 through 9 and then never see the plan implemented. A few years after the planning, someone comes along and says, "We need a strategic plan." You can expect a chorus of groans and exclamations: "We did that already!"

To be effective, a strategic plan must be a living document, and it needs to change and respond to the changes that occur both within and outside the organization. That's why this final step in the development process doesn't end—not as long as the plan remains in effect. This is where the plan is maintained and updated.

Using the steps in this book helped you avoid the agony often associated with the lengthy process of traditional strategic planning. Even so, you certainly expended a lot of effort in completing the plan—effort that should not now be wasted. Strategic plans are

STEP 10

meaningless if they're not kept up-to-date. A maintenance plan that gives directions for continually updating and refreshing your strategy helps keep it alive.

In this final step we'll address these topics:
- setting and following a plan review schedule
- identifying common maintenance triggers
- using a comprehensive process for continual plan maintenance.

Case Examples: Maintaining the Plan

The following case examples illustrate how two companies maintained their strategies through updates and rewriting.

Updating Core Elements of the Plan

Axion Inc. faced a serious reorganization when a large share of its product line became obsolete. The product line fizzled because a competitor created new technology that was more advanced and more customer friendly. After the company furloughed more than 30 percent of its workforce, it began an effort to reposition itself in the marketplace. A review of its strategic plan revealed that the mission, objectives, goals, outcomes, and tactics needed to be updated to reflect the current environment. After some anxiety about keeping a strategy flexible enough to meet dynamic circumstances, Axion modified the mission, objectives, goals, outcomes, and tactics of its strategic plan. As a result of this maintenance, Axion employees have a much better understanding of the organization and where it's going in the future.

Success Breeds Commitment

A large insurance company, Safe4U, developed a strategy one year ago. In an effort to create a more efficient workforce, the strategy included many tactics related to technology. The director of strategic planning found it difficult to convince the CEO that a new strategy was needed, but when it was implemented, the CEO was impressed with the results. Now that the plan has been yielding positive results for a year, the director has had no trouble at all gaining the CEO's approval to maintain the plan regularly every 12 months using a detailed process. The CEO believes this maintenance will save time and money in the long run.

Scheduling Plan Reviews

Maintaining your strategy need not take a great deal of time. It may require as little as a couple of weeks every three years. If a complete overhaul is needed, however, it may take as much time as developing a new strategy. How long it takes depends on how much change has occurred since the plan was first developed or last updated.

If change has been minimal—if you have the same customer demographics, offer the same types of products and services, and hold the same mission—then the maintenance will focus mostly on new goals and tactics. But if your mission has changed, it's another story—that kind of change demands a large-scale strategic planning effort.

There are two basic methods for scheduling a strategy review. The first is to schedule it like any other task. The second method is to identify a set of maintenance triggers and review them on a scheduled basis.

Example 10.1 demonstrates the first method of scheduling, indicating how often each component of the plan will be reviewed and the specific date of the next scheduled maintenance. Even if you choose to set a definite schedule for plan reviews, any type of significant change in the business climate should prompt an immediate review, without regard to the standing schedule.

STEP 10

EXAMPLE 10.1

Sample Maintenance Schedule

Strategy Component	Maintenance Schedule	Next Scheduled Maintenance
Mission statement	8–10 years	January 10, 2017
Vision statement	3–5 years	July 31, 2012
Values statements	8–10 years	January 10, 2017
Strategic goals	1–3 years	November 1, 2008
Strategic objectives	1–3 years	November 1, 2008
Strategic outcomes	3–5 years	October 31, 2009
Plan tactics and schedule	1–3 years	November 1, 2008
Measures	1–3 years	July 31, 2008

If your organization is fairly stable, with a durable product line, strong and immutable core values, and a customer base that hasn't changed over the years, this method of scheduling maintenance will work well for you.

But if your organization is in a dynamic industry, and especially if it's young or small, you're probably better off using the second method to prompt a plan review. Regularly looking at internal and external change triggers will signal when one or another component of the strategic plan needs to be updated. We'll discuss these triggers later in this step.

A set schedule for component review is based on expectations at the time the strategic plan is finalized. But nothing is so constant as change in any organization. Therefore, those people who are responsible for overseeing the strategy or the planning group and for ensuring that the strategy is meeting the organization's

STEP 10

current needs and circumstances should meet every six months to consider the business environment and decide if something essential to the organization's continued success and future plans has changed. They should review the existing maintenance schedule and alter it in any way they think is beneficial. Generally speaking, a maintenance review should occur every six months.

Identifying Maintenance Triggers

Maintenance triggers are internal and external changes that may indicate a need to update the strategy.

External triggers are changes occurring outside of the organization that might affect its strategy. Examples of external triggers include economic changes such as increasing oil prices, geopolitical upheavals like armed conflicts and terrorism, or rapid changes in technology such as faster computers that can increase customer expectations. These types of changes will most likely require a review of the whole strategy.

Internal triggers are changes that take place within the organization. For example, a corporate reorganization may affect the strategic plan; economic changes influence what the organization does; and changes in goals or objectives, or in organizational systems, processes, or procedures, affect the tactics and the relative order of their importance, the evaluation metrics, and potentially the evaluation instruments themselves.

Being aware of change happening around you, both inside the organization and beyond its walls, is half the battle of staying current. Organizational change is the most frequent internal trigger, and it's important to ensure that your strategy continues to be linked to the business. If you look back over the changes that have affected your organization in the past two years, most likely you'll find that the changes occurred in one or more of the following areas:

- technology
- customer sophistication

STEP **10**

- marketing approaches
- global expansion
- human resource base
- resource availability
- the local, national, or international economy
- competition
- leadership or structural changes.

In thinking about these triggers, it's easy to see how quickly things change year to year. Responses to business drivers often change business needs, so the organization's strategy must change to meet the new business need.

Identifying the external and internal triggers that are affecting your organization is crucial to keeping your plan active and productive. Worksheet 10.1 lists key factors in your strategy that may need to be addressed and revised in the presence of an external or internal trigger. When you've linked an existing trigger to the factor it's affecting, it will be easier to review the strategy and make appropriate changes. The worksheet is designed to be used with numerous triggers; no need to complete a separate worksheet for each change trigger.

With the triggers and affected factors identified, and a decision made about what needs to change, the maintenance process described below will help limit the time spent on doing the maintenance.

Using a Detailed Process to Maintain the Strategic Plan

Many organizations schedule maintenance into their strategy as they design it. They know that, with rapid changes in technology and global expansion, the company will naturally evolve over a period of three years or so and it will be necessary to readdress the strategy as a whole.

The first step to reviewing the strategy is to review the mission statement as it exists. Does it still define "who the organization is,"

WORKSHEET 10.1

Identifying the Impact of Maintenance Triggers

Instructions: In column 2, identify any internal or external triggers that affect the currency of the strategic factors listed in column 1. In column 3, describe how those triggers affect that factor. An illustrative sample is included.

Strategic Factor	Maintenance Trigger	Impact on the Strategy Component
Business drivers	*Increased cost of oil has increased the cost of transporting goods to distributors.*	*This external trigger is forcing the company to review how best to decrease shipping costs. It may necessitate reengineering how and when distributors receive the products and possibly the whole notion of having distributors versus shipping directly to end-use customers. Obviously, this would be a huge change to the business model and would require a review of the strategy.*
Business drivers		
Organizational mapping		
Data findings		
Customer needs		

continued on next page

Worksheet 10.1, continued

Strategic Factor	Maintenance Trigger	Impact on the Strategy Component
Business needs		
Learning needs		
Financial needs		
Cause-and-effect relationships		
Mission statement		
Mission objectives		
Tactics		
Resource requirements		

Priority of resources

Timeline

Budget

Measures

Communication plan

its purpose, its customer base, its product line and services, how it offers and delivers its products and services, and what the environment would be if the organization did not exist? The mission statement often is stable unless there have been drastic changes to the organization's customer base, product and service base, or the marketplace in which it operates. Typical events that affect mission statements are large mergers or acquisitions, deep global expansion, and sweeping leadership change. In most cases, a mission statement is stable through several strategy rewrites.

After the mission statement has been addressed, it's important to identify what has changed for the organization and how that change might need to be addressed through strategic objectives. The most efficient and effective way to do this is to look at maintenance triggers. (Refer to the most common external and internal triggers we listed above.)

After the triggers have been reviewed, it's important to review the measurement results that were previously set. Is the organization on track to achieve those results? Does more work need to be done? Has a result been scrapped? Are new measures needed?

With the information on the mission, triggers, and measures in hand, the outcomes, goals, and objectives can be addressed. First, what outcomes, goals, and objectives from the previous strategy are still relevant and in progress for the new strategy? Then, what new outcomes, goals, and objectives need to be developed for the organization and documented in the new strategy?

At this point, you should have enough information to identify what maintenance is needed. Is it simply readjusting the existing strategy? Or do you need to create a completely new strategy? Or does the need fall somewhere in between those two extremes?

If out of this review there is a bit of "outcome overload" (or more than five clear strategic outcomes for the strategy), you will need to prioritize the maintenance needs. This is where the tools used in chapter 7 will be useful again in prioritizing.

When the outcomes have been prioritized, you're ready to kick off the strategy maintenance by revisiting the necessary steps in this book to develop a new or revised strategy.

Tool 10.1 condenses this process information into a handy reminder format.

TOOL 10.1

The Maintenance Process Described

Maintenance Process Step	Description
1. Review the mission statement	Ensure the mission statement still identifies what is unique about the organization and defines its purpose and the market it serves. Determine if any changes in the operations of the organization have altered the mission and should now be reflected in the statement.
2. Identify the maintenance triggers	Determine what has changed internally or externally and if these changes have triggered a need for components of the strategic plan to change as well.
3. Review the measurement results regarding the strategy	Determine if the organization is on track and meeting the desired measure. If not, decide what needs to be changed within the strategy to ensure that the measures are met, or decide if the measures themselves should be revised.
4. Review the strategic goals, objectives, and outcomes	Determine if the goals, objectives, and outcomes have been met. If not, why not? Does something need to happen to achieve the desired outcomes and the corresponding goals and objectives? Identify what new outcomes are necessary for the health of the organization.
5. Identify the maintenance needs	From the four previous steps, identify the most likely maintenance needs.
6. Prioritize the maintenance needs	Determine which of the maintenance needs are the most important to the organization and its health, and which are of least importance.
7. Kick off the maintenance	Initiate an updating of the strategic plan by defining the scope of the maintenance. Revisit the 10-step process detailed in this book as appropriate to the maintenance.

STEP 10

If a conscientious and careful review of circumstances shows that a complete overhaul of the existing strategy is not needed, then the changes to the strategy should be documented in an addendum that can be attached to the original strategy document. The addendum should include the following elements:

◆ summary of identified triggers
◆ brief description of how those triggers have affected the current strategy's tactical plan
◆ description of changes to the current strategy, by tactic
◆ description of and plan for new tactics to be implemented as a result of environmental or situational changes
◆ evidence of the need for or rationale behind the changes themselves
◆ updated list of required resources, budget, and timeline.

NOTES

GLOSSARY

Advocacy mapping: Identifying who in the organization will be a sponsor for the strategic plan and what's in it for them to do so.

Advocates: The people in the organization who support the development of a strategic plan. Advocates may be customers, stakeholders, business partners, or sponsors.

Balanced scorecard approach: An evaluation method, created by Robert Kaplan and David Norton, that consists of four perspectives (customer, learning, business, and financial) and is used to evaluate effectiveness.

Business drivers: The internal and external factors that affect an organization's strategy and therefore its business needs. An example of an external business driver is government; regulation or deregulation forces changes in competition or the overall business environment. An example of an internal business driver is technology; technological innovations create opportunities or needs for changes in information storage and processing.

Business need: An organization requirement identified by examining business drivers and deciding how the company will respond to an external or internal force. Examples of business needs include increased competitive advantage, increased sales, and more rapid development of new products or services.

COCOMO: A specific cost model for estimating the number of person-months required to develop software.

Communication plan: An overall plan for publicizing a strategic plan, including key messages, target audiences, timeframes and communication points, required resources needed, materials to be developed, and distribution dates and mechanisms.

Cost model: A template for calculating the budget or line item costs of implementing a tactic.

Data coding: Grouping data into categories for analysis either by strategic outcome or by a specific topic in the strategic plan.

Data collection: The gathering of information through focus groups, interviews, surveys, and research as required to develop a strategic plan.

Data collection instrument: A written document (such as a survey, observation worksheet, or a focus group or interview guide) used to gather the data needed for developing a strategic plan.

Descriptive statistics: Numbers that summarize how questionnaire items were answered. Descriptive statistics include frequency, percentage, cumulative frequency, and cumulative percentage.

Expected results: The business outcomes to be realized when the tactics identified in the strategic plan have been implemented.

Falsification principle: The principle at work when agreement with a data finding is reached through the influence or opinion of a dominant player or someone with seniority.

Maintenance: Periodic updating of the strategic plan based on changes in the organization, new business needs, industry trends, and the overall economic environment.

Maintenance triggers: Internal and external changes that may indicate the need to update the strategy; for example, changes to the organization structure, changes in technology, or the entry of new competitors in the marketplace.

Marketing message: A message that promotes realistic expectations about the strategic plan.

Mission objectives: The direction the organization, group, or department will take, and the goals to be pursued. The objectives communicate the ultimate purpose and intention of the entity.

Mission statement: A brief declaration of why the organization, group, or department exists. It provides the foundation on which the entity will build its products and services and identifies to whom it will offer them.

Organizational structure: An organization's reporting relationships and decision-making processes.

Pivot table: An interactive table of summarized data that can organize data in different ways for easy comparison and analysis.

Preexisting information: Data already available from organizational or outside resources that can save time in data collection.

Priority setting: Deciding which tactics, resources, outcomes, or results are most important to the organization or merit more attention or resources than other elements in a strategic plan.

Reliability: A characteristic of the data that indicates to what extent they are consistent and dependable.

Resource prioritization: Rank-ordering the resources needed to execute the strategic plan, using cost models or linking resources to business drivers and objectives.

Risk management: Identifying a situation or problem that may put specific plans or outcomes in jeopardy, and then organizing actions to mitigate it.

Sponsor: The executive or manager who is supporting the strategic plan, who provides financial approval for it, and who navigates the political waters on its behalf.

Strategic plan document: Written record of a strategic plan, usually consisting of an overview, strategy charter, description of the current environment, research findings, tactics, roles and accountabilities, key performance indicators, and recommended next steps.

SWOT analysis: A scan of the business environment to identify the organization's strengths and weaknesses and the opportunities and threats it faces.

Tactical plan: A detailed list of actions to be taken over a three- to five-year period to achieve specific desired results or outcomes. The plan specifies required resources and intended timeframes.

Tactics: Actions that will lead to specific desired results or outcomes.

Thematic analysis: Arrangement of data by themes, ideas, or topics to make analysis of the data less difficult.

Validation: Confirmation or corroboration of something, such as a business need or an identified opinion or recommendation.

Validity: A characteristic of the data collected that indicates they are sound and accurate.

Values statement: A declaration of the traits, behaviors, or qualities that will define or characterize the organization's actions and those of all who represent it.

Vision statement: A declaration describing where the organization is going or what its future will be. This type of statement is more idealistic and inspirational than a mission statement.

INDEX

A

accountability: assigning, 14–15; for data collection, 72; for marketing, 28, 30–36; for tactics, 186–88

advocates, 18–21, 23–24, 27–28; *see also* business partners; customers; participants; sponsors; stakeholders

Analyzing Collected Data (Step 4): case examples, 110–12; overview of, 3–4; timeframe, 45

B

background research, 95, 98, 100–3, 109

balanced scorecard, 127–29

brainstorming, 139, 147

business drivers, 64–67

business information: checklist, 71; for developing a strategic plan, 47–48; financial indicators for, 55–58; resources, 53–54; safety guidelines, 70–71; for specific outcomes, 49–52; *see also* data

business partners: in collecting data, 86–88; defining questions, 21; definition of, 17; and mission, vision, and values statements, 140–41; *see also* advocates; customers; participants; sponsors; stakeholders

business plans, 6; *see also* strategic planning

business results, 179, 181, 183–84, 194–95

C

case examples: Step 1 (Laying the Foundation), 7–8; Step 2 (Scanning the Business Environment), 39–40; Step 3 (Collecting Relevant Data), 74–76; Step 4 (Analyzing Collected Data), 110–12; Step 5 (Stating Mission, Vision, and Values), 134–37; Step 6 (Pri-

oritizing Needs and Identifying Risks), 162–63; Step 7 (Designing and Validating Tactics), 176–77; Step 8 (Prioritizing Tactics and Resources), 190–92; Step 9 (Documenting and Communicating the Plan), 213–15; Step 10 (Maintaining the Plan), 230–31

checklist, 71

Collecting Relevant Data (Step 3): case examples, 74–76; overview of, 3; timeframe, 44

commitment: gaining, 22, 129–32; of individuals, 14–15; kickoff, 40–42; lack of, 22; through communication, 219–20

communication plans, 28–29, 219–22, 226–27

cost analysis, 210

cost models, 200, 203–9

customer results, 181, 184, 192–94

customers, 16, 20, 86–88, 140–41; *see also* advocates; business partners; participants; sponsors; stakeholders

D

data: analysis process, 121; background research, 95, 98, 100–3, 109; coding and sorting, 112–17; collection accountability, 72; collection and customers, 86–88; collection methods, 83–86, 92, 95; defining the collection scope, 80–81; organizing, 113, 116–17; planning for collection, 76–79; resources for collecting, 103–5; validity of, 103–4, 106–7; *see also* business information; findings

department planning, 10–12

Designing and Validating Tactics (Step 7): case examples, 176–77; overview of, 4; timeframe, 45

Documenting and Communicating the Plan (Step 9): case examples,

Susan Barksdale and Teri Lund have worked together for more than 15 years providing businesses with consulting services and expertise in strategic planning, evaluation, and performance improvement. They are known for their practical approaches to improving business processes, performance, and the bottom line, and have been praised for their ability to translate complex theory into easy-to-understand applications. They have worked to improve performance and strategy for many organizations, including HP, Intel, Microsoft, Allstate Insurance, Wells Fargo, US Bank, The Capital Group Companies, TVA, ETHOS Development, Sun Microsystems, and Intelsoft Texhnologies.

Susan Barksdale has been a consultant for many large corporations for the past 23 years. Prior to this, she managed training and consulting departments for two financial consulting firms. She holds both undergraduate and graduate degrees from the University of Wisconsin (UW). Before entering the performance improvement field in 1979, she was a psychotherapist at a major medical center and in private practice. Barksdale also taught communication and behavior management courses at UW–Milwaukee.

Teri Lund has been an external consultant for the past 15 years, after holding management positions for Barclays Bank, Kaiser Permanente, and Sealund and Associates. She has a bachelor of science degree in education from Montana State University and a master's degree in international business and finance from New York University. Lund has in-depth experience in managing projects, implementing technology solutions, and determining and measuring return-on-investment.

Barksdale and Lund repeatedly have been invited to present their work before international audiences at professional performance improvement conferences, and their writing has been published in several periodicals.